AN ARTIST CROSSING DISCIPLINES

CARRIE IDA EDINGER

An Artist Crossing Disciplines Copyright © 2017 by Carrie Ida Edinger

A Currier & Rice Publication

United States of America

For More Information:
Carrie Ida Edinger
www.carrieida.com

First Edition

Designed by Kelly M. Carter | fourdogcreative.com

Library of Congress Control Number 2018907674

ISBN 978-0-692-14623-1

for Phyllis Marie Finley

AN ARTIST CROSSING DISCIPLINES

CONTENTS

INTRODUCTION:
THE ABSENCE OF THE ARTIST'S VOICE

At times crossing disciplinary boundaries has metaphorically reminded me of the basic American driving guidelines forbidding crossing the double yellow line on the roadway. The double yellow line is meant to be a boundary for driving safety and awareness of a curve or incline in the road. These are examples of when the driver's vision of oncoming traffic can be obscured. More than once, my vision has been obscured in the process of crossing academic disciplinary boundaries and those were the complex moments of wanting to veer back into the safety of my fine art background.

From my research and experiences, I have found that the artist's voice is under-represented when it comes to specific research methods and the perspective artists have of their practice crossing disciplinary boundaries, such as using anthropology. Following the lineage of the 1960's artist writing from the cultural turn of late twentieth century media, my text is focused on the development of knowledge pertaining to theory and practice from my twenty-first century experiences. The knowledge from my human experience is the basis for the inquiry with higher education and art practice.

Artist writings have long histories representing both experimental and theoretical approaches. A notable shift is from the emergence of specific styles of art such as public happenings, pop art and conceptual art in the late 1950's. For me it was art historian, Dr. Kristin Stiles, who used an example of a standard joke between art historians that describes the tension between who, art critic/ historian or artist, has the authoritarian voice over a text and the work of art. The joke is "The best artist is a dead artist," suggesting that dead artist can't talk back. Her argument states that artist writings are material evidence from an art activity as well as the artist's human experience from social and cultural conditions of a specific timeframe.

My discovery of artist Adrian Piper gave me an example of an artist who included individual experiences within her writing and art practice. She did talk back to cirtics in her two-volume text that pursued a broader perspective and rejected the autobiographical label, which made it clearer to me how an artist's individual experience can reflect the current social and cultural conditions. The intent of Piper's writing was for a broader cultural scope, which included personal experiences relating to her identity within the higher education environment and the 1960's art world. Piper demonstrated this by taking into consideration her personal and nontheoretical approach to her text that grapples through her artistic creative process, along with her observations of discriminatory actions in social settings.

I view her text as an example of an artist stating her perspective from a specific time frame. As I have referenced the tensions of the authoritarian voice for the artist as writer-practitioner in the beginning of this section, the challenges are in the form of either being alienated or the misinterpretations of the individualized writing. Piper's race and background differ from my own, but what is stimulating is that she was willing to take the challenge of representing her artwork with her own artist's voice.

My research with specific genres of academic writing does reach beyond the singular notion of the art historical background of the visual arts. I have investigated the anthropological methods toward text. This is in regards to consider the language for my cross-discipline reading audience. One format is the ethnographic writing style, which can represent research methods such as participant observation, interviewing and other participant techniques that aid in the development of content for the writing. An ethnographic text representing the authority of the anthropologist has a similar structure that relates back to Dr. Kristin Stiles views from the art discipline of who has the authoritarian voice.

With the investigation of the lineage of art and anthropology, my focus was concerned with the process and activities that are involved with crossing these disciplinary boundaries. I discovered that other contemporary publications pertaining to the subject of art and anthropology tend to be identified from the anthropological perspective. As I read these publications, I wanted the inclusion of a larger number of artist's voices within these anthropological writings. I kept thinking to myself, what were the artist's thoughts on their own cultural background, the environment, and the collaboration as a whole.

This has reminded me of anthropologist Roger Sansi's question, "Perhaps it is more interesting to ask or see what use artists make of anthropology. That would imply a different question: rather than asking if they are using anthropology properly, one could ask what are they using it *for*." I view Sansi's question as a response to the debate between anthropologist and artist. The debate is over whether an artist's engagement with anthropological methods and faithful representation of a community is either as an expert or as an amateur.

The purpose of my first person writing is to expand the twenty-year-old dialog concerning cross-discipline practice between art and anthropology. The distinct content is from my perspective as an American woman artist whose work has conducted the integration of digital media and methods that are borrowed from anthropology. I view my individual experiences as a reference to how I crossed the double yellow lines of academic boundaries rather than a step-by-step research guide with a singular inquiry. From each specific discipline background, I have included the approaches from each discipline that I have drawn from, while evaluating how new media has altered those disciplines structures for the process of my *Collection Project*, which I reference throughout this text. My monograph contributes to the development of defining the artist's role with the production of knowledge beyond a standard visual means to interdisciplinary practice.

ART AND

ANTHROPOLOGY

INTRODUCTION:
FROM ART TO ANTHROPOLOGY

"How did you go from art to anthropology?" In some way this form of inquiry has been interjected into my discussion, while I am describing my interdisciplinary practice. The emotional reaction from the participant that I am conversing with can range from a sense of wonderment to a tone of disdainfulness. I am assuming the critical reaction comes from thoughts that I have abandoned my fine art background. Depending on the participant's reaction from the conversation, the dialog either ceases or proceeds a little further in detail.

From several of these various conversational experiences that are either at academic conferences or other art related programming, I have never asked the people who are reacting in such a critical way why they view my research experience this way. Conference environments typically offer brief interactions with new people instead of allotted times for fully detailed conversations. If I had lengthier time allowances, I could have been exposed to some middle ground from my conversations.

Since I was caught up in the moment from those conversations and have experienced the reaction several times, I have begun to reflect on these short conversations. From my previous experiences, I am willing to develop any future conversations to gain more insight from these interactions. Currently, I can only make assumptions by some of the last statements that ended the previous conversations.

One example of a statement is "You invested all that time learning a specific fine art technique then disregarded it from your practice." While this statement does have a slice of truth to it and I did set aside segments of my fine art practice during the development of my *Collection Project*, I have never publicly announced that I am distancing myself from art or my own contemporary art practice.

From my previous studio art practice based in a printmaking and fibers background, I have created several bodies of artwork through out the early stages of my artistic career. There has been an evolution with my image making process. The image style has gone through a transformation of abstract two-dimensional forms to sculptural forms. In the working process of creating my artwork, I have questioned the outcome of a finished artwork. This is not a formal critique of my creative progress, but I manage the multiple stages of my visual observation as an individual artist within my own art practice. The reason why I use the phrase individual artist is because each artist has his or her own working methods. I came to a main point of inquiry, which was that I have exhausted my fine art methods for image making.

This thought brings the dialog back to that original inquiry of going from art to anthropology. From these conversations, I have been introduced to a diverse range of perspectives concerning an individual artist pursuing cross-discipline research. In the current standing from the types of conversations that I have described, they are individual responses to the concepts related to my process of interdisciplinary practice. In many ways, I personally view this as being similar to an individual response to a finished piece of art. Basically, some people will hate it and some might love it. As for any gray areas to these conversations, the Art and Anthropology section is intended to expose those gray areas from my process of borrowing anthropological methods, along with the integration of text. This section is not intended to be a resolution to the opposition from previous conversations, but as a reference to my practice-led research pertaining to a cross discipline approach.

THE ARTIST'S POSITIONALITY

I have borrowed the anthropological writing approach of drafting a positionality statement to expose my specific Western culture background and the accounts of my experiences. Positionality is significant to the creation of knowledge that comes from research and relates to people and experiencing a specific culture. The anthropological approach tends to concern an anthropologist actively unlearning his or her primary culture to have the ability of moving outwards from that culture. The significance of practicing this method in fieldwork is to confront positionality and learn the new embodied knowledge. This process that exposes new embodied knowledge can lead to the identifications of the differences from other cultures or from researching the differences of the American subcultures.

Understanding these differences is completely grounded in self-awareness. Self-awareness leads to positionality, which is considered in broader terms beyond common identity characteristics. Positionality can refer to family and individual struggles that impose socialization and self-development. My artist positionality statement is from the perspective of my experiences from academia and how my childhood-embodied experiences helped me to redefine material culture concepts. My childhood background has an important role with my perspective of the transition of objects. This is because my parents kept and actively partook in the Great Depression era values that they grew up with.

Borrowing autoethnography methods enabled me to "unlearn" or analyze my fine art discipline culture. From my personal perspective, there were absences in my fine arts discipline and academic background with concepts relating to social engagement and everyday objects. What was sparse in my studio art practice was the skill set needed to articulate about my art on a broader social scale. The art mediums I was utilizing did not aid in the representation of objects in a transitional state.

These questions and transitions in my art practice didn't happen until my second year of graduate school where I was pursuing my Master of Fine Art (MFA) degree. Prior to graduate school, I was a practicing artist for ten years. My definition of practicing includes making artwork with printmaking and sculptural methods and exhibiting my art in the Mid-Atlantic region of the US. I was also a visiting teaching artist to art centers and at risk youth community centers. I have held a couple of art administration positions at a commercial gallery and contemporary art center. I attended graduate school to change my art practice methods.

My investigation of cross-discipline approaches with anthropology began with an additional year of graduate school to study visual and material culture in the Contemporary Art Theory program at Edinburgh College of Art in Scotland. Included below are a couple of paragraphs from the methodologies section of my thesis, *Transformation of Personhood Through the Concept of Work*, which was written in the form of an autoethnography investigating my work process as an artist, instead of critiquing a completed art object.

FROM MY THESIS

I put aside the majority of my fine art background to study visual and material culture at Edinburgh College of Art. The experience of attending an art school with no intent to use the studio facilities gave me an 'outsider looking in' perspective. This experience was the beginning of including anthropological methodologies of 'fieldwork' observation. This was at times very awkward, especially after just graduating from an MFA program based in studio art practice. With this experience, I was able to examine the social, cultural, and economic aspects of being a working artist in the fine art discipline culture using methodologies from other disciplines.

Reflecting upon my past and present experiences with gallery and museum space, fine art funding, and the American aspects of art culture, the social structures therein became more relevant. Through my courses and assignments I was able to practice and reflect upon the use of these approaches. The inclusion of a portion of my graduate thesis was for a broader point of view in my research that was achieved in my graduate studies. I consider this academic experience a foundation in the development for my art-based research to reach beyond a single discipline.

After graduation from the one-year program, I continued my research in anthropology, material culture, museum studies, and social histories. In the initial development of the *Collection Project*, I would again consider the visual representation of an object. Before considering how to investigate a cross-discipline approach and similar to what I began to learn in graduate school, I set aside elements of my fine art background. This was to begin the *Collection Project* in an interdisciplinary manner.

Digital media is a new inclusion to my practice and for my purposes has extended the concepts of visual representation of the functionality of objects. With my choice to "unlearn" my fine art discipline, I do not consider myself a trained anthropologist. I had to personally learn about visual anthropology and how to conduct interdisciplinary research before I applied the borrowed methods to a project. My life long learning approach develops and revitalizes my art practice. While my positionality statement has been focused on a specific time-frame of my academic studies, which was supplemental to the development of my cross-discipline approach to the *Collection Project*, I am going to proceed beyond academia with other aspects from my individual experiences that have contributed to the *Collection Project*.

My original concept for the *Collection Project* of objects in transition is spurred from my childhood household daily life structure that came from my parents Great Depression era values. The Great Depression was from 1929 to the late 1930's and was the most widespread worlds economy depression of the twentieth century. World War II began in the late 1930's and in American culture there were many rationing and recycling efforts to provide resources for the war effort. Both of my parents lived in this time period from mid-childhood to young adult life and my parents in my childhood home environment continued these habits of rationing and recycling.

My everyday experiences through childhood in my American East Coast household revolved around collecting and reusing of objects and materials as well as making many utilitarian objects. Some of the utilitarian objects that were made out of necessity were quilts, kitchen linens, various furniture, and articles of clothing. The household routine consisted of food production, maintaining the small vegetable garden in the spring and summer months, and performing household maintenance, fixing problems with objects and materials from various scrap bins. This idea of "fixing" was actually a temporary patch until the actual piece that was needed could be afforded. Sometimes that patch had to be mended several times until the item wore out. My childhood household was in a continuous cycle of sorting, altering, and mending, which indicates my personal interest with the activity or functionality of an object beyond a "fixed" traditional museum context. This all has evolved to the concept of social engagement between people and objects that I have investigated in my material culture research for the *Collection Project*.

BEGINNING THE ETHNOGRAPHIC PROCESS WITH TEXT

Text is part of the preliminary stages of my field methods, which have enabled me to examine the social interactions between objects and myself. The type of ethnography I employ for the majority of my research is experimental or autoethnography. Writing as a method of documentation has become primarily used to focus on this detail engagement to produce a video clip for a specific collection theme. This has enabled me to establish viewpoints for framing the subject matter within my creative process of the project, but also to obtain a broader knowledge of everyday objects pertaining to activities and functionality.

My fieldnotes are derived from the personal activity with an object and my research usually does not focus on a specific environment pertaining to that object. Text enables me to record the step-by-step process of the activity. Text-based fieldnotes are the construction and production components to the social reality of a specific field that is being observed and experienced. Since fieldnotes can be considered as private text, they are rarely made open to the public and are often being edited for a published academic text. My fieldnotes are similar to writing from the subconscious to note each stage of the social interactions between object and myself.

The collection theme that I used to begin this method with was the *Can Opener Collection*, which was the first video clip collection. To the right is the written documentation of an Easy-Open Lid food can. It is an everyday activity that the majority of us are familiar with and seems to be done in seconds.

EASY-OPEN LID DESCRIPTION

The right hand is securely grasping the main body of the can. The tin can's cylinder shape it is easy to grasp. The right hand reaching for the tab blocks the long thin rays of light that bounce across the shiny surface of the lid. With a starting position of the pointer finger on the tab and the thumb on the outer edge of the can the pointer finger's nail begins to lift the tab from the surface. The pressure from the hand to the fingernail along with the hard metal surface pulls the nail slightly from the finger. This induces slight physical pain causes a reaction to slip the end of the finger under the tab. The pointer finger pulls the tab to the vertical position away from the lid of the can. This new position of the tab breaks the seal of the easy open lid. A suction noise occurs when the seal is broken and the center of the can swells and rises with the air entering the can. The pungent smell of condense soup is pushed out of the can with the entering outside air. With the tab bent up vertically a very small section of the lid is bent inward. This exposes the sharp edge of the lip of the can. The hand repositions with the pointer finger in the opposite direction and the thumb in the center of the can. Now all the pressure is on the thumb while the pointer finger is lifting the lid from the can. The tendons tighten across the back of the hand as the motion is carried through. The sound of metal releasing from metal does not last long in the quickness of the motion. The condense soup odor becomes stronger as the opening is enlarged. The thumb's position moves from the outer edge of the can to move upwards with the pointer finger. The thumb contributes to the grasp on the tab during the final separation of the easy open lid. The hand carefully twists back and forth with a final sound of the metal edges scrapping together to confirm the lids removal.

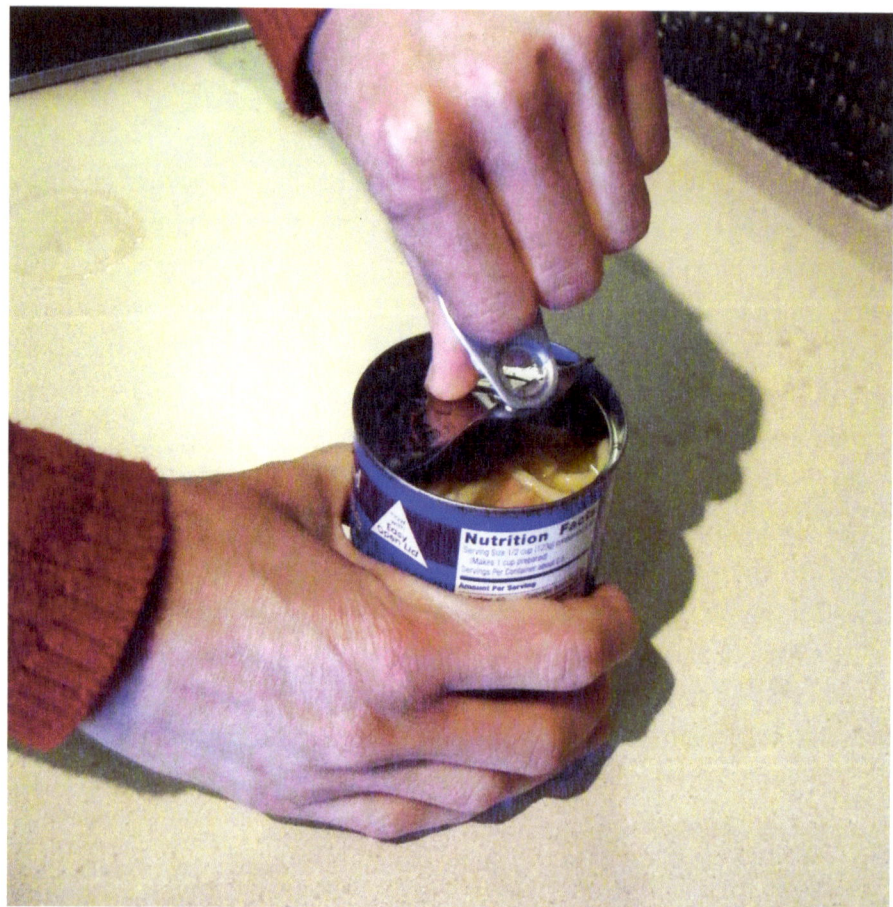

Fig.1. This research image accompanied text pertaining to an easy open lid for the Can Opener Collection. The image was published on a blog with the preliminary research for the collection. Digital Image Creation Date: 2011

My example includes forms of sensory ethnography within this text method, which pertains to the senses of the participant with their object and their bodily involvement. In my fieldnote example, the detail is placed on tactile experience and how the range of motion of the fingers opens the metal lid [Figure 1]. For an expansion of ethnography methods to be considered as part of participatory practice, anthropologist, Sarah Pink, proposes to rethink the traditional roles of participant observation from the anthropology discipline to a multisensory experience. Fieldwork should be framed from ideas of learning and gaining knowledge from the embodied, emplaced, sensorial, and empathetic.

Documenting the human perspective during the engagement of an activity with an object with written language has offered the ability to observe in real time instead of from memory. In my previous studio-based art practice process, I would begin a project from memory of an object or experience. An example would be my 2010 drawing series. The drawings visually represent some of the objects from my parent's scrapbins that I grew up sorting through. This drawing series is depicted with a realistic visual style compared to my other series of artwork. The process of these drawings was to personally reflect on a specific object while I drew it.

My memory was based from a time-period that ranged from 25 years ago. Many of the objects no longer exist or are no longer in my possession. I did not have the opportunity to examine them since they were not archived. The objects were discarded in some capacity from either everyday living or being exhausted from an unorthodox use. My memories were from moments of a utilitarian purpose or in a specific space. The accompanying visual image is of *Blown* [Figure 3], which is an example from the 2010 drawing series. The object represented in my drawing is a household electrical style fuse with a cracked glass front that illustrates the fuse has blown. This style of household electrical style fuse predated the current circuit breakers used in household circuits [Figure 2]. This drawing doesn't depict the fuse completely in a realistic manner. The screw portion of the fuse in the drawing is replaced with the drawn layers of overlapping fabric that stand in for that section of the object. Since the objects are from memory, portions of other objects are drawn in relating to the overall form of an object. From my childhood memories, this visually creates how the objects were adapted for other functions within the household.

Utilizing the ethnography process of text has provided me with the ability to have a "slowed down" analysis concerning the social interactions between people and myself with the activities related to objects that tend to be overlooked in everyday occurrences. Archiving my preliminary field notes of the activities for the *Collection Project*, before capturing the social interactions by means of video, conveys that my research is not dominated by a visual method. Even though visual images play an important role in sensory ethnography, using a variety of mediums for practical and permanent documentation, such as text, implies research and experience from my ethnographic process.

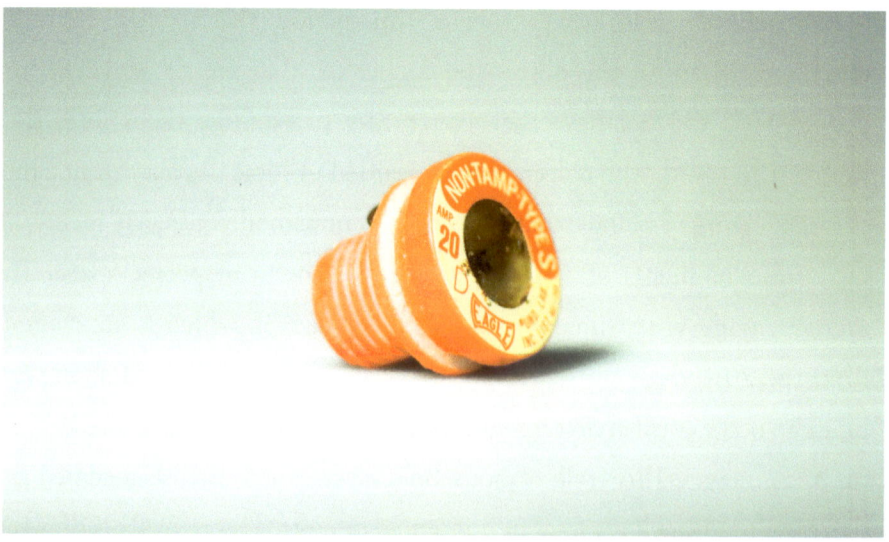

Fig.2. Household electrical style fuse

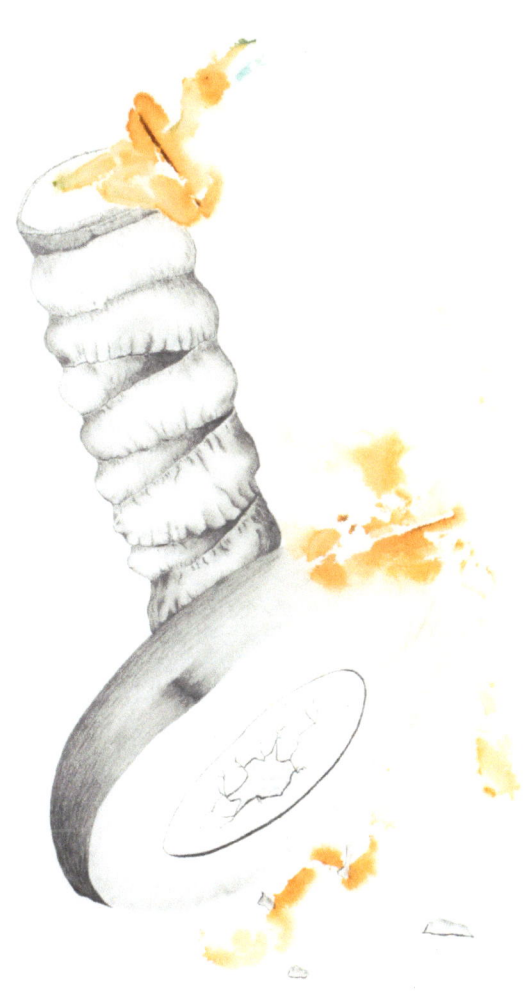

Fig.3. "Blown" graphite, rust, and dye on paper 30" x 22" 2010

BORROWING METHODS AND ETHNOGRAPHIC ROLES

To inform my collection project, I have considered the ethnographic roles of participant and ethnographer. I consider these roles "working roles" in my art practice and research. My working roles are for a practical sense and have structures within my research to obtain a fresh perspective pertaining to the functionality of objects. These roles enable me to reveal knowledge concerning the sensory experience and the stages of the interaction with an object to contribute to each collection theme.

The concept of performativity is a very new addition in my practice. While I have described these actions as roles that are working through the ethnographic process, this method has enabled me to move away from art language concerning "personas" that refers to performance-based art. By borrowing these anthropological methods, I can present a non-fictional concept of the social interactions with American Western culture objects with the combination of text and borrowing the working role experiences from the anthropology discipline.

Since, I participate in both roles for the majority of my research, I consider these dual roles as contributions to the establishment of viewpoints. These viewpoints are considered in framing the subject matter for the video clips in the collection. I use the term "dual roles," because I participate in both (participant and the ethnographer) for the majority of my research toward the social interaction between objects and myself. As the roles change rather quickly through my ethnography process, I am the ethnographer when I am documenting by the means of text concerning the step-by-step social interaction and I am the participant when I am engaging in the activity involved with the object.

With my research, I am concerned with how I consider field methods and the ethnographic roles that inform my collecting process. When I am employing both roles, it is to focus on my body's interaction with the object without including an environment. These two viewpoints are brought about with the methods of observing my activity with the object, note taking, and self-interviews that focus on the senses. This all references back to my ethnographic process with text. Writing as a method aids in designating the two roles in my ethnography process. This is accomplished in the documentation of the step-by-step process, which refers back to my "slowed down" analysis concept.

In wanting to capture the embodiedness of my experiences with objects, I related to Amanda Coffey autobiographical ethnography method. This method is utilized with writing, which captures the fieldworker experiences as well as the extent to the connection of the social and cultural experiences of fieldwork. By acknowledging the dual roles within my autoethnography, I have established one of these methods that are connected to the commonalities between (auto) biographical practice and ethnographic representation. The connection is toward the production of the authors or ethnographer's voice being present in the text. The debate within the anthropology discipline over the rejection of conventional ethnographic writing styles and the ethnographic truth from these specific methods, offers the opportunity to a broader debate that concerns the purpose and presentation of the importance of a specific voice or voices to the personal narrative within theory and practice.

My *Collection Project* does have a multiplicity of voices. This is established with the interviewing of other participants and documentation process. When I am observing and interviewing a participant I am only working in the ethnographer role. Other participants have contributed their knowledge of specific objects that I do not use. A couple of examples are part of the *Mouth Collection*, which is smoking a cigarette and a participant having his mustache trimmed. *The Trimming of the Mustache* video from the February 2013 addition of *The Mouth Collection* is an example concerning detail descriptions of ethnographic roles. This example investigates the two participants social interaction experiences with a pair of scissors.

This example provides two forms of knowledge revealed from sensory experience with the act of trimming a mustache. The two participants are the gentleman with the mustache and myself. The gentleman with the mustache didn't want to be identified. He will be referred to as John to be respectful of his request. The perspective from John is in regards to the social interaction with the scissors being used to cut his facial hair. My perspective is of being engaged in the act of cutting hair with scissors. I have the control over the action of the scissors and John is the passive participant.

A section from my field notes, written in the form of an interview explores the sense of touch with facial hair from both participants' experiences with the use of the scissors.

Below are two examples from the interview.

SECTION FROM THE INTERVIEW WITH JOHN

"It is hard to sit still, because when the hair is cut it touches and tickles my nose and face. This is ongoing through the cutting."

SECTION FROM MY OWN SELF-INTERVIEW

"With the scissors in my right hand, I begin to cut the coarse hair. Carefully I trim along the upper lip. Opening and shutting the scissors in a repetitive action."

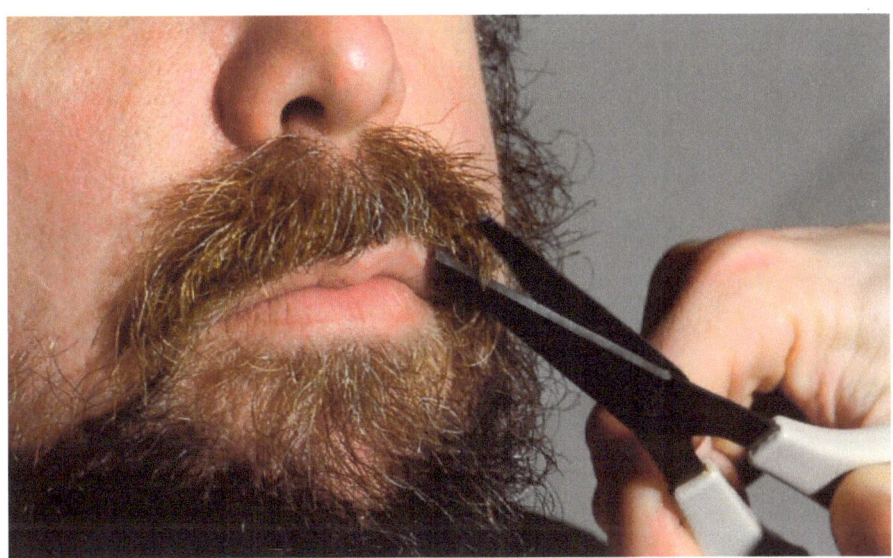

Fig.4. Still from February 2013 Video Clip Mustache Trimmed, from the Mouth Collection

The sections offer an acknowledgement of how documenting these roles can expose multiple perspectives before the staged recording process of the video clip for the collection theme. In addition, this example demonstrates when I am the ethnographer, which occurs as a singular role of when I am observing a participant. My experiences from the dual role activity gave me insight to ask questions pertaining to the participants and their senses as related to their objects and bodily involvement. This type of fieldwork leads to the final video documentation of the activity.

THE LIVED EXPERIENCE AND THE COLLECTION

My inquiry pertaining to social engagement for the *Collection Project* is taken from the perspective of the human experience with objects. During my investigations of phenomenological anthropology, I came across an essay that described the ethnographic study between the human body and a single object. Shawn Lindsay described his *Hand Drumming* essay as an experimental style essay. I remember how he expressed in his introduction that his essay was only a success if it offered other ethnographers an insight to enable the integration of practical knowledge into their disciplinary tool kits. Lindsay's research implies that practical knowledge is essential for the subject (person) to have knowledge of an activity with an object. The *Hand Drumming* essay is one of the first writings that I could associate with my own borrowed anthropological methods concerning objects.

Practical knowledge was categorized as a tool to enable him to acknowledge his own experiences of learning to perform with the musical instrument called a djembe drum. While Lindsay's essay integrates the discipline of music with his research, from reading about his experience with a singular object, in this case a drum, I could consider my own investigations of everyday objects to form my collection themes. I consider Lindsay's essay as a resource, especially the sections that focus on the "embodied" or social conditions from his experiences with practicing the drum and group performing. These sections not only refer to the body's praxis, but also specific senses that are involved, such as hand-ear coordination.

The one difference between Lindsay's investigation and mine is he was in the beginning stages of learning how to "drum" the djembe drum. I am forming my collection from the current knowledge of others and myself with specific objects that are already integrated in everyday life. Through out the *Collection Project*, the most common representation is of the single social engagement between a person and an object. While my lived experience is being depicted visually by means of video, the activity being presented enables the viewer to have a reference point to the social engagement. I define a lived experience to be a routine activity with an object that I have represented in my ephemeral collection. The challenge of representing a universal American everyday object is in how the viewer will consider each lived experience. The viewer usually reacts with his or her own subjective lived experience to each object during the viewing time of the video clips.

During the first couple of years of the collecting process, I observed several viewers subjective perspectives. My observations of the viewers were with possible participants or during a friendly conversation with a peer from my sharing of the current state of the *Collection Project*. I would sit and listen, while taking in their reaction to each video clip of a specific collection theme. From my observations, I have come to determine it is a combination of the medium of video and the detailed consideration of presenting the social engagement that aids in the viewers attention to the specific objects. I took a mental note of these experiences, but I did not consider how to include these viewing perspectives within the collecting process.

In the spring of 2013, I had the opportunity to "restage" one of my collection themes pertaining to color with a color-blind perspective. The *Interaction with Color Collection* presents the role that color represents within specific types of activities, characteristics of an object, and the human body as an object. These are my concepts for the collecting and documenting process to this collection theme. From the current additions of the *Interaction with Color Collection*, the color-blind perspective provides a personal experience with the visual representation of color.

The color-blind participant's name is Harry. Harry first realized he was color-blind when he was going through testing for aviation training in the United States military in 1965. Color codes have a large role in military aviation signaling. Being color-blind limited Harry's advancement in his training. Less than ten percent of the male population is color-blind. For women it is rare, but still possible since color-blindness can be inherited.

Harry's perspective on the *Interaction with Color Collection* is not a color vision test. During the time-period of the restaging, I requested to Harry to put a side, the best of his ability, the social standards he has acquired with color in his everyday living. A common example of color used as a social standard would be the placement of the colors red and green on an American traffic light. These colors are also among the most questionable for the color-blind person to identify. The limited ability for the color-blind person in determining certain colors can be due to the shade (light to dark) of the color.

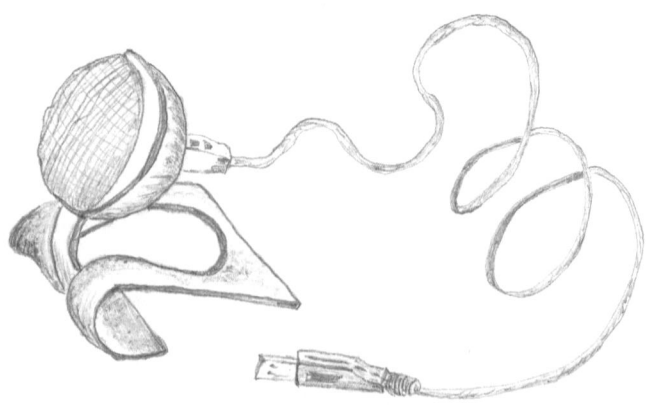

Fig.4. Sketch of microphone used for recording session. May 30, 2012

After Harry recorded his perspective of the collection, we had a conversation about two distinguished visuals and the prominent color associations. The one video clip is of a person coloring with crayons in a coloring book image of a tree. Harry explained to me as he observed the video that he sees green as the crayon color. He continues with his explanation that the image of the tree also directs his thoughts about the color; because he has been told several times that a tree trunk is brown. In this example the image presented in the video clip has a role of persuading Harry to comment on his color choice.

The *Interaction with Color Collection* has been restaged with the depiction from various media forms rather than the tradition concepts to restaging a tangible object-base collection. Audio is used to present another visual perspective of the collection theme [Figure 5]. The verbal response of the participant, Harry, was recorded while he watched the February 2012 thru April 2013 additions to the collection. The original sound of the video segments was removed. This act enables Harry's voice to be prominent and to restage the collection with his visual perspective.

The audio from the video clips of the collection was not the only original content removed. The title pages introducing the collection were altered to introduce the restaging concept. The "new addition" title pages had also been removed from the whole video collection. Deleting these title pages was intended to remove my collecting process idea, which provides about a half hour of a different experience of the collection from Harry's color-blind perspective. The alterations of the video's technical elements created the "restaging" presentation. I view my "restaging" as an extension to Linday's perspective of his essay by the inclusion of media and cross-discipline research methods. Harry's color-blind perspective questions cultural norms while exposing his adaptation with the identification of color to American everyday objects. As I was writing the blog posts for this "restaging" of the collection, I shared my text with Harry before it went live. This is not only important for ethical purposes of practice-led research, but to continue the dialog if it is needed for accessing multiple meanings.

ART AND ANTHROPOLOGY WITH AGENCY

From the beginning stages of my art and anthropology research, I investigated the anthropological perspective of art objects. In his anthropological theory of art, social anthropologist, Alfred Gell wasn't interested in the hierarchical status of an art object, but instead the social agency. He developed a theory using four terms: index, artist, recipient, and prototype, to order and classify generalizations of these social relationships with an artwork. Gell scientifically charted out the primary and secondary agency of these relationships between the artists and spectator of the artwork. Gell's anthropological methodologies of a social process were relevant to his "action-centered" approach to art. From Gell, my research for the subject matter of art and anthropology evolved to looking at how other researchers approached their process and activities that were involved with crossing these disciplinary boundaries for contemporary projects.

Amanda Ravetz is a visual anthropologist who has crossed the boundaries from being trained as an artist. Her co-edited book with Anna Grimshaw is entitled *Visualizing Anthropology*. Both of these visual anthropologists are committed to practice-base ethnographic work. This type of visual anthropology research can range from a gallery installation to the photographic essay. Ravetz and Grimshaw have established in their publication how art and anthropology methods have the ability to actively pursue research from a practice-led inquiry that is demonstrated through a range of perspectives with individual essays.

The act of making is explored through Tim Ingold's anthropological analysis with the creation of knowledge from the disciplines of anthropology, archaeology, art, and architecture. The investigation of these disciplines alone is not what drew me to Ingold's research, but also that both disciplines art and anthropology have the absence of the creativity to the productive process that bring the artifacts themselves into existence. Ingold's theory is to link art and anthropology by the connection of their practices instead of a work of art as an object that is usually conveyed by the conventional study in anthropology of art with an ethnographic analysis of an object.

Relating back to my *Collection Project*, this is an example with how art and anthropology are part of the productive practice. I have grappled with putting aside my art discipline to allow a different approach for the beginning stages of my creative process. Instead of anthropological methods leading the research analysis, Ingold includes art to be regarded as a discipline that knowledge has the ability to grow from within the making process. My perspective is for another discipline's approach, because I have exhausted my fine art visual knowledge from my previous art practice.

In giving my presentations at both art and anthropology conferences the knowledge that I presented on borrowing methods does have some critics. As for the evaluation of knowledge from these methods, Sociologist, Patricia Leavy evaluates the knowledge by a "no one-size-fits-all" model. The difficulty with setting standards for the evaluation of knowledge with arts-based practices has to do with the similarities of art and the social sciences. Both of these practices have a focus on a holistic approach, which includes methods such as problem formation and solving, an element of reflection, along with identifying and explaining a specific research process. The strengths of art-based research serve interdisciplinary endeavors by enabling a particular view through the discovery of processes.

She continues by stating that defining any research achievement is to conceive the connectedness to the research purpose and how the methodological approaches expedited the research objectives as well as stressing the importance of communication of specific findings. Her assessment issues are based in working with innovated approaches. For Leavy, the research community should reevaluate "good research" and the level of expertise in a particular art form. This would alter the standards to other assessment questions pertaining to what does the work reveal. Refering back to the "no one-size-fits-all" model, her outline for reconfiguring the assessment of art-based research does consider the value of the project within the terms of the research and the educational role. Intertwined within her context is how do researchers consider the artistic craft and adaptation of it, along with learning the discipline's historical and methodological background, which the practitioner is crossing into.

I do agree with Leavy and Ingold over the importance of evaluating the artistic process in cross-discipline research and the challenges that come along with the renegotiation of evaluating art-based research. From my artist perspective, my fine art background is a crucial part to why I began to inquire with the expansion of methods in my studio art practice. I had to live through my earlier fine art experiences to understand the absences within my individual practice. These embodied experiences are the kind of inquiries Ingold is arguing for with his relations between thinking and making toward the variation of the process. However, instead of viewing knowledge from each separate discipline in the creative process, I consider the borrowed anthropological methods and the digital mediums to be working very closely together in the stages of my creative process, which have placed action toward my interdisciplinary practice with the development of knowledge.

The conclusion of Roanna Heller's essay *Becoming an Artist-Ethnographer* does acknowledge how researchers do struggle with the tensions between the artistic process and social research methods. These artworks and projects should be regarded with more time allotted for the development of a foundation for the project. I can clearly relate with Heller's closing argument from my own artistic experiences with the complex moments of combining a cross-discipline approach.

Attending academic conferences has been one opportunity to build peer relationships within the anthropology field, along with moving beyond my book-based research. Since the *Collection Project* has had more of an individual approach my challenge was maintaining a current dialog on contemporary projects. My query with crossing disciplinary boundaries and learning about other peer's projects led me to write an *Anthropology News* column entitled *Crossing Disciplines: Art and Anthropology*. My objective for the column was to keep a broad enough subject matter between the two disciplines by including artists, anthropologists, and museum studies that crossed over these disciplinary boundaries. The one-year column offered a writing practice with a different format of text that has enabled me to have insight to a diversity of methods, along with cultural and academic interests. From this style of engagement what has emerged is the sharing of knowledge by exposing a specific method or the material and conceptual making process to cross-discipline projects.

REDEFINING

AN EPHEMERAL

COLLECTION

INTRODUCTION:
THE COLLECTION AND THE INTERNET

I n my United States Mid-Atlantic region, my experience with cultural institutions comes from their background of nineteenth century hierarchical structures. These structures presented and focused on the original owner of a specific collection and that the collection is usually housed in their estate that has become a museum. These collections seemed quite distant to my relationship with everyday living. The focus of these objects was related to a specific time-period and the categories of decorative arts and design.

The museums and their cultural background are steeped in a long tradition of the du Pont family. The du Pont family has been known as a wealthy American family and for their global corporations that produce material sciences from the twentieth century. My disconnectedness to the du Pont's collections and social background is derived from the differences in our social economic backgrounds. My background can be categorized from a traditional idea of working class, but I am college educated and do not have a prominent family heritage. Considering this regional cultural environment within my museum studies and material culture research, I have gained awareness of the focus that is placed on an object's provenance and the absence of public presentation of collections that have a broader scope to everyday living.

It was important to me to obtain a broader knowledge of American Western culture everyday objects that regarded the objects beyond a fixed idea of how they are exhibited in traditional museum collections. My thought process was brought about from my personal background with various objects in transitional states and my visits to the social history museums in the United Kingdom. Upon my first couple of visits to Scottish social history museums, I couldn't help but notice the display of everyday living. The exhibits weren't focused on the style of design from that era, but how people actually lived in their homes and community. Most of the displays I did view in the beginning were from the World War II era. As I read the educational information that accompanied the display there was mention of how materials were rationed and what could be commonly found in a working class home. It was the first time that I could personally relate to a museum display, because of my familiarity with my parents background with depression era values from the same time period.

While this discovery during my graduate studies offered a new vision of objects in a museum context, I was still missing the pieces to answer my research questions of how to represent objects in transition. For my Internet-based collection project, I have investigated and implemented interdisciplinary methods to maintain and archive an ephemeral collection. My interest in interdisciplinary practice for this *Collection Project* came from the activity of borrowing methods from other disciplines that enabled me to develop supplementary conceptual material. These methods contribute to my visual practice in the forms of media such as video clips and print media objects.

The significance of my Internet-based collection is to present the social interaction between people and objects. The concept of social interaction between people and objects is to present the functionality of the interaction instead of putting the main focus on the object alone. The collection project has themes that organize the concepts of the social interactions between people and objects. The introduction of the collection themes is presented by media categories that aid in the formation of the collecting process. *The Mouth, Can Opener, Screwdriver, Interaction with Color*, and the *Smell Collection* have video clips that represent the collection themes.

The subject matter for the video segments ranges from specific types of activities with everyday objects, to the human body as an object. The title clips at the beginning of each collection video introduce the title of the theme. A second title clip introduces the context of the theme that is described in two or three sentences. This introduces and engages the viewers with the theme as well as the visual representation. The inclusion of a written form of content has expanded the visual representation opportunities by offering the viewer an insight to the context of the collection themes.

The malleable characteristics of the Internet have contributed to maintaining the collection themed additions that were added each month. Currently the Internet has reached a status as an everyday communication medium. The fluid boundaries of the Internet's virtual space offer an infinite arrangement for digital content. Through the evolution of the *Collection Project* website, I managed the site as a virtual destination used to follow a collecting process instead of a marketing tool for my artistic practice.

From the fall of 2011 through 2015, I considered social and cultural aspects of the current Internet era, such as the transitional phases of web browsers and the inconsistent availability of bandwidth frequencies to people with lower social economic backgrounds. I have chosen to present the videos at a lower resolution for a quicker download time and provide easier public accessibility to the collection themes. My focus was not heavily based in technical, but instead the development of accessibility with the Internet platform and how my digital media research could be extended with these concepts.

I utilized the Internet's characteristics to alter the status of the collection each month during my collecting process. This screenshot image contains the collections web page [Figure 6]. I have arranged the most recent additions for the latest month in the top row, while the bottom rows are laid out to group the collection in their entirety. This webpage presentation is for new and recurring visitors to the site to have access to the different stages of the collection. The Internet redefined my collection status as well as the concept of public accessibility.

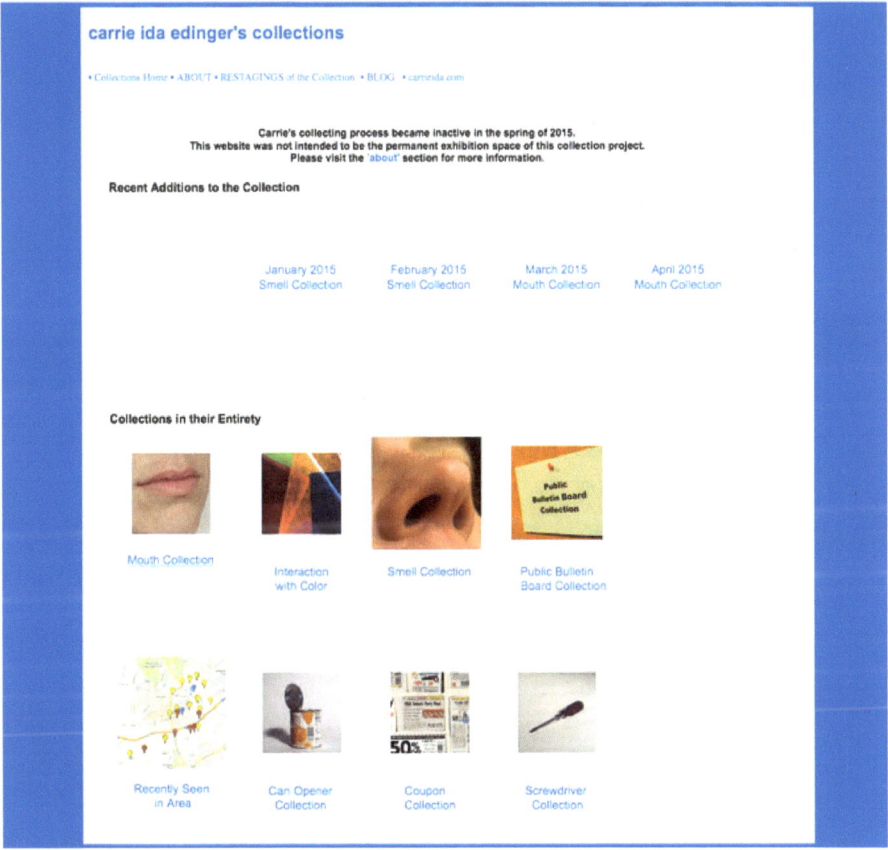

Fig.6. Screenshot of the collections webpage. The web design of this page evolved from the activity of maintaining the additions that were added to each collection theme. The top row is where the recent additions for the latest month were posted. The bottom rows are the collections in their entirety. Source: carrieida.com/collections.html last modified 2015.

One of my main accomplishments with my *Collection Project* was in having the ability to collect and visually present the functionality of everyday objects or objects within a specific transitional state. I did not consider the project's website to be a permanent exhibition space, but rather a platform to present the evolution of the collecting and curating process. These ephemeral objects, print media coupons, video clips, and digital images, are archived separately from the main website. This is for future opportunities for others who are interested in "restaging" the collection in a different manner or for research purposes.

TRANSITION OF MEDIA

Taking notice of the visual change in the print media coupon form is what began the collection project. This visual change is from the traditional coupon to a QR Code. The process of collecting and forming a collection with print coupons contributed to the continual analysis of the transition of print media culture. There is a transition in the social interaction between a consumer and coupons, which made me consider how coupons would be collected for discounting purposes. Instead of a tangible printed object changing hands it would be a transfer of electronic digital information.

Print media is one of the conventional ways to define an ephemeral object in a collection. The print media coupon represents a type of tangible artifactual object of the twentieth century. The form of the coupon is in an altering state of being in its tangible print media form to being in an intangible form that is stored digitally in an electronic device. My collecting process for this collection is transferable to the context of private and institutional collections by means of archiving, management, and exhibiting the collection.

The process of collecting and forming a collection with the coupons will contribute to the continual analyze of the print media culture's transition.

As an artist, I have collected the printed coupons using material cultural methodologies such as social anthropology and archaeological curatorship, rather than using fine art methods of visual representation as printed images, I have employed these material culture methods of 'fieldwork' and archiving that have enabled me to classify the coupon in broader cultural terms.

My interest in forming my *Coupon Collection* began when I noticed an increase in the digital coupon codes in my local print media ad circulars. I have considered the difference in participation with the exchange of coupons from the print media form to an intangible form stored on an electronic digital device, as in a smartphone. This transition of social interaction between a consumer and coupons made me consider how coupons would be collected for discounting purposes. Instead of a tangible printed object being exchanged it would be a transfer of digital information. My focus is not for the collection to be intended for a utilitarian manner in the process of consumption, but as artifacts that once contributed to the social interaction of exchange.

The beginning stages of my collecting process consisted of receiving and clipping the coupons from the ad circulars. The nature of the collection is to collect from the print media form of the coupon, which I acquire locally by means of postal mail, hand delivered advertisement circulars and purchasing of a local Sunday newspaper.

The typical information to be found on a coupon can be seen with the savings amount, name of manufacture or retailer, guidelines, barcodes, images of the product, and the expiration date. This date is my focus of the coupon, because it finalizes the social interaction of the person and the discount of a good or service. I group the coupons by the month of expiration. This indicates they have become a tangible artifact of the social and communicative process of trade.

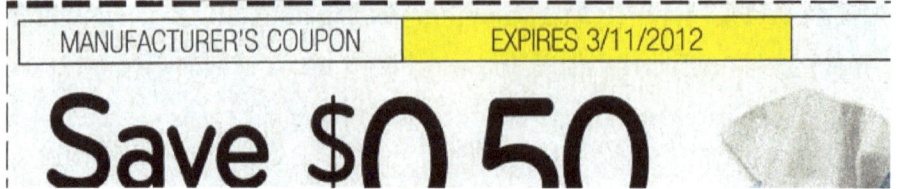

Fig.7. Detail of Coupon Expiration Date Highlighted in Yellow Box From the March 2012 Expiration Group of Carrie Ida Edinger's Coupon Collection

From the anthropology discipline, Anthropologists, Anna S. Agbe-Davis and Alexander A. Bauer explore the idea that what has been neglected in artifact studies, is the full understanding of indexical meanings in relation to social and cultural relations. An analysis of artifacts of trade in purely economic terms only offers part of the meaning. From this trade process the print media coupon is seen as a form of communication. This form of communication is being presented in the process of trade in an intangible sense, such as traditions, ideas, and values. These intangible forms are demonstrated in a broader social and cultural process that establishes and maintains connectivity between participants. The coupon is part of the distribution of formal and informal communication within a community's social context. In the act of consumption, business agendas and personal affairs are being circulated as much as goods and services of trade.

The coupon's temporal time period presents several circumstances other than the current economic times. The expiration date contributes to the limited time frame of social and cultural circulation [Figure 7]. The tangible print object (the coupon), with a visible expiration date, demonstrates Agbe-Davis and Bauer's broader artifact studies of intangible communication and connectivity between participants and trade. The role of the coupon in the social interaction of trade is presented by a group of artifactual coupons and organized by the month of expiration. Each grouping reflects the cycle of this temporal time period for the social interaction of the trade process.

Presenting another form of an analysis, anthropologist, Daniel Miller, whose theory is that an artifact should begin with its existence as a physically concrete form. The physicality of the artifact not only provides the significance in cultural construction, but it is also the bridge between the mental and physical worlds. I will focus on Miller's inquiries of *Artifacts of Space* and *Artifacts and Time* to present my coupon collection as artifacts beyond what tends to be the standard economic viewpoint.

For the coupon's utilitarian qualities to occur, it usually needs the social interaction of a consumer to carry out the process of redeeming it and the retailer or manufacturer's expiration date on the coupon to finalize the trade process. Miller uses the example of artifacts tending to leave an impression on society. These exotic qualities are a symbol of space. He uses this example to describe prestigious imported goods and the access to highly priced goods in competing status systems in the population. The coupon has no higher standards of exotic qualities, but is a temporary object of discount that is distributed to the majority of the population, which offers them access to high or low priced goods.

The timing of the social and cultural circulation is temporal. Miller refers to the use of rituals and sacred objects from a certain time period. These objects act as texts or symbols that transpire as interpretations instead of "true" meanings. Miller does consider more than just sacred objects, by discussing how mundane objects do obtain some kind of biography and their significance may be radically altered by this added information.

The coupon can be a symbol of frugal living or thrift, but it contributes to the activity and advertisement of consumption. A study from Inmar Inc., a company that processes coupon transactions, reports that after nearly two decades in decline the use of coupons has increased in the US, since the recession of 2008. This change in economic times has brought the use and idea of savings to be used in present times. Miller refers to objects and their temporal symbolism by how long they stay in fashion with their cultural meaning. This is determined by how the object stands for time and time controlling what the object stands for. The present time makes the object fashionable, but with the movement of time it is enviable to become unfashionable. As the United States economy moves out of a recession the coupon can become unfashionable to use in a new economy.

A 2008 MSN Money article, *The Death of the Coupon*, describes a different perspective from the 2010 Inc.com article pertaining to the coupon being back after two decades. The MSN Money article's stance is that electronic discounts by means of smartphones and electronic accounts linked to retailers loyalty card numbers will shift the tangible object form of the coupon to an intangible form of discounting. The article focuses this shift towards the idea of convenience for consumers and retailers. Through this transition, the retailers gain more information about buying habits of customers and demographics, while customers upload discounts from the internet onto their electronic devices with the possibilities of using the discount more than once without needing multiple copies of the tangible printed coupon.

The MSN Money article demonstrates Miller's argument of the temporal symbol of an object, by showing the coupon evolve from a symbol of savings to a means of distributing the concept of mass consumption. Besides representing the temporal symbol the article also demonstrates the concepts of space and time of an object moving out of fashion. These aspects of intangible forms of discounting by convenience and the transition of new forms of media support my argument of the artifactual print media coupon. This is demonstrated by how the print media coupon exchanges hands as a symbolic object of discounting in the trade process.

To form my coupon collection, I borrowed from present material culture methodologies, along with the concept of archaeological curating and archiving. This is utilized in conjunction with the management of this collection that has been obtained through contemporary means of print media circulation. I researched another source for collecting and curation methods, Susan M. Pearce begins by referring to what the nature of an archaeological collection is. Considering her reference with the 18th Century time period in England, the idea of collecting artifacts begins as a private collection that is acquired by a public institution. Prominent gentlemen collected artifacts from their travels and exchanges for reasons of rarity of an object, craftsmanship, and according to intellectual rationale. The majority of the private collections were passed into the possession of museum institutions. These early collections from collectors with Renaissance prestige tend to have developed an antiquarian value on artifacts and not studied for the material culture aspect of society. Pearce refers to the developments through the 1960's and 1990's that include the nature of material culture as part of the meaning of the study of artifacts.

Pearce's three distinguishable forms of activity that contribute to the curation of an archive are to understand the nature of a collection, artifact-based research projects, and the exhibition. Even though she has referenced these activities to be practiced with a museum institution collection she states that her book is not to be conceived as a manual of archaeological curtorial practice, but instead it concentrates on issues of theory and practice. These concepts are now in the forefront of curating and future development. My research and collection practices will appropriate Pearce's forms of activity beyond the museum collection and I will employ them to develop an archive of the *Coupon Collection*.

Procuring new acquisitions is one aspect of the management of a collection. Pearce indicates the active relationship between curator and the archive, which involves taking into account historical documentation and the conservation of the collection with museum policies. The coupon collection is organized and stored in special boxes for conservation purposes. I have organized the *Coupon Collection* with information cards for each month of expiration. This card contains the information of community location and the tally and dates of the new acquisitions. The collecting process has been documented on hard copy form as well as cyberspace. The cyberspace presence contributes to my activity with the coupon collection that usually is not present with a physical exhibition. This public presence is significant to maintain and acknowledge a collection status since an institution does not maintain the *Coupon Collection*.

It is demonstrated on a smaller scale that the *Coupon Collection* is managed very similarly to an institutional collection. The archiving structure is different in the process by the means that there is not an official curator or a museum institution collection management policy. These institutional terms can imply a form of persuasion to define the idea of a collection, but can they imply new theories and practices for objects as artifacts in contemporary society? Since the majority of museum's collection's tend to be derived from private collections it can be indicated that private collections have as much value in developing context and interpretation for present day artifacts.

My acknowledgement of Pearce's form of activities has developed a foundation for my collection practice and context. The foundation is appropriate to enable me to analyze and organize my *Coupon Collection*. Obtaining acquisitions from a continually evolving public realm creates an interchangeable form of the concept for a collection. My artifact-based research demonstrates Pearce's concepts and activities towards understanding the nature of the coupon as an artifact, which actively pursues theory and practice toward the formation of the *Coupon Collection*. The coupon as artifact has acquire a status in time and space by a four-year time frame of my acquisitions, public access via the Internet, and the transitional process of print media culture.

THE EVERYDAY AND REDEFINING
MATERIAL CULTURE

Repurposing various objects is what defined ephemeral in the early stages of my life. This was part of my everyday living situation. I will reflect on a few selective everyday activities and the embodied experiences that have impacted my material culture research. Both of my parents taught me how to create utilitarian objects. My mother's role in this process has had an impact on my investigations with the activity of objects in everyday living. In my youth my mother passed down to me the knowledge of traditional women's material practices, such as cooking, sewing and crafting. Examining the engagement of a gendered based material world can discover the intellectual, social and cultural contributions from women's material practices.

I came across the book, *Women and Things, 1750 – 1950*, about halfway through writing this book. As I read through the first couple of chapters, all that came to my mind was a wish that I had read this book as an undergraduate student. The context would have helped me with a broader understanding of traditional women's material practices. I would have used this knowledge while I was completing my Bachelors in Fine Arts degree; then I would have been able to articulate about my body of artwork beyond the Fine Art definition of craft. As I shuffled the book pages back to the beginning of the book and found the copyright date to be 2009, I realized the book hadn't even been published when I was an undergraduate student. *Women and Things* is comprised of a group of essays that demonstrates how material culture concepts are related to the significance of the interactions between the subject and the object. The collection of texts intends to expose women's productive labors within the process of making and manipulating of materials instead of the role of consumers. One of the main objectives is how women's material practices place the focus on how objects were conceptualized, produced, circulated, used, and exchanged; these action based concepts serve as a foundation to rethink material culture theories between subject and the object.

Some of these objectives are parallel with the focus of my *Collection Project*. Certainly with this book, I could explore the traditional women's material practices that my mother passed down to me, such as the sewing production process. The activity of sewing was taught to me by means of hand stitching and employing a sewing machine. My mother was very meticulous with her stitching and the production process as a whole. By her example, I learned how to organize the production process and follow through with a high standard of craftsmanship. With needle in hand and by pricking the edges of the fabric to bind them together, I have embodied this repetitive act for hemming or constructing a cloth object.

The production process consisted of the lay out for a cloth object as well as preparation of the materials and specific tools. Conceptualization tends to begin from these early stages within material practices, but conceptualizing is implemented through out the entire production process. Some of those activities include making alterations to an object, along with the mending process. My mother would mend linens and clothes to extend their longevity and the cloth objects would be placed back into the household's everyday circulation with a well-placed and durable patch [Figure 8].

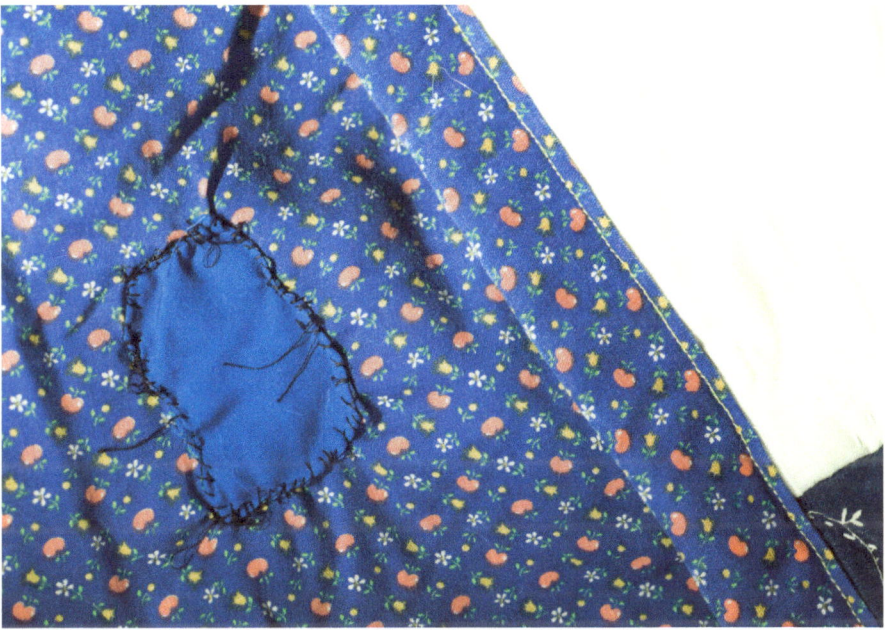

Fig.8. A quilt with a dark blue patch that was sewn on by Carrie's mother.

As part of the production process organizing the materials and tools for the construction of the object was heavily emphasized. In preparation of everyday wear within my household, the cloth object was constructed to have durability and the type of cloth was usually chosen from a practical sense. Some of the objects were created as decorative objects for the home, such as table scarves or doilies. This relation to women's productive labors within the material production process is one example of the social significance that does refer back to one of the main objectives for the rethinking of material culture theories between subject and the object, which for this example would be the materials of the making process.

The process didn't stop with learning about sewing techniques. These cloth objects played a major role in the functionality of everyday living. Quilts are an example from my mother's material practice. Even though these objects had a limited circulation distance, the quilts were circulated on a seasonal need in my home. While these quilts kept me warm in the winter months, the majority of the materials that formed a quilt held another structure of circulation. Some of the quilts where made from leftover cloth that was kept in my mothers scrap bins. Instead of relying on a conventional pattern, she would improvise how these cloth scraps would form into a quilt. My mother's name for this specific style of quilts was *Crazy Quilts*.

This circulation of cloth and the construction of various objects does hold personal memories. The majority of cloth that created many *Crazy Quilts* was used in the production of another cloth object. As a little girl and even now looking at those quilts I can pick out which cloth my mother used to create something else, such as making a dress for me or herself. Through out my elementary school years my mother made the greater portion of my wardrobe. I wore them out or grew out of the articles of clothing, but I remember specific patterns or colors from my childhood. My mother's *Crazy Quilts* are material objects from the scraps of specific clothing production. In addition, these acts are from her "waste not want not" aesthetics from the depression era.

Exchange is the last concept from how women's material practices place a focus on objects. I approach exchange in two different ways from my personal exposure of women's material practices. There is the exchange of knowledge from my mother concerning the sewing practice and in a tangible sense, there are the cloth objects that my mother created as well as a few from my maternal grandmother. I do not use many of the objects in relation to how they were used in my childhood home. I now care for the objects from a preservation perspective of transitioning into family heirlooms rather than the everyday use that they once had. In relation to my material culture and museum studies, the cloth objects that were made by my mother are artifacts that represent traditional women's material practices.

By presenting the social and cultural significance of woman's engagement with material practices it offers the opportunity to document women's history, along with placing material culture studies within the research realm of theory and practice for art-based research. Through my example of my mother's sewing practice, social meanings can be demonstrated by the activities from the production process of an object. The example from these material categories fall under concepts related to the mundane, the knowledge from the materials, the production of an object and how women manipulate the material world within the understanding of specific social meanings. All these examples are significant, because my embodied experiences from women's productive labors are my foundations with material practice. These processes would appear in my undergraduate studies of academic fine art. My transition to material culture began from my previous experiences with a fine art studio background that has a foundation in studying fine art techniques and art history.

My material culture studies and embodied knowledge of women's material practices are integral to the development of my artistic career and research of everyday objects. Instead of becoming a specialized field, the notion of rethinking material culture does lead academic research into concepts of risk taking with hybridization of methodologies. There is a need to expand an interconnection between various disciplines that could integrate material culture theory, which would lead to interdisciplinarity. My example of an individual perspective and the adaptation of knowledge through the hybridization of academic, social, and cultural experiences offers the opportunity to re-evaluate how the artistic process and individual background develop the cross-discipline research for material culture theory.

"RESTAGING" IN THE PHYSICAL AND VIRTUAL SPACE

To define my collection, I have referenced museum terms, but digital technologies extend the idea of what a collection can be. This has posed the challenge of how to "restage" my ephemeral collection within different physical environments. This research and practice has enabled me to establish methods toward digital curation and restaging concepts for the management of the *Collection Project*. For the *Collection Project*, curation methods are conducted in a broader sense rather than the conventional four white walls of a gallery space and an existing museum collection. With the time-period of the project, I considered my curation methods to be in a varying state that changed according to a specific media's collecting process and the space for a "restaging."

Physical objects or artifacts tend to be the focus within a restaging concept. The only tangible objects that are part of the collection project are in the *Coupon Collection*. The *Coupon Collection* began by acknowledging that the form of the coupon is in an alternating state between print media form and digitial form. This collection is exhibited on the *Collection Project* website by means of numeric tallies that were organized by each month's expiration date. The restaging of my collections artifactual object was in one of the public display cases at the Newark Free Library [Figure 9].

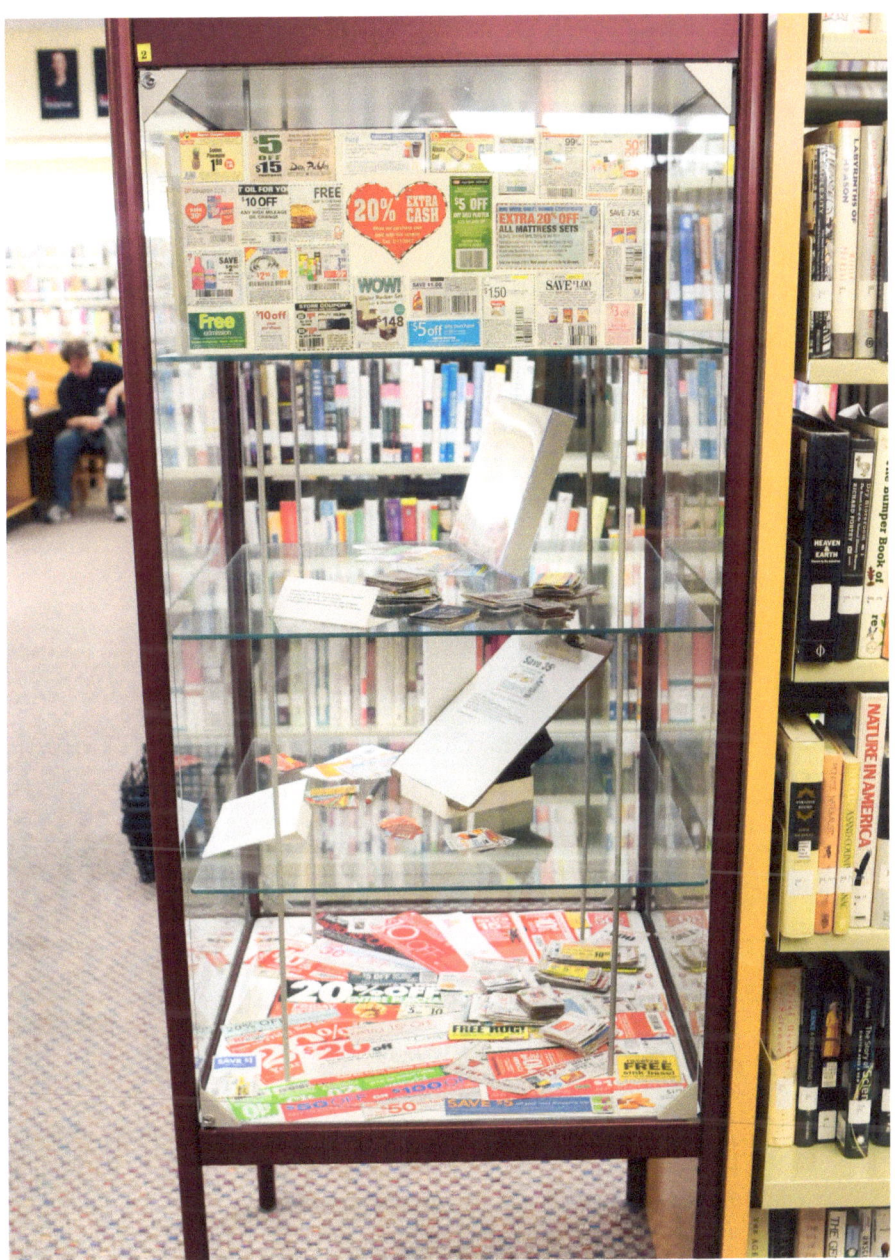

Fig.9. Portion of the Coupon Collection was "restaged" in the Newark Free Library display case in Newark, Delaware for the months of June - August 2012.

In Newark, Delaware USA, the Friends of the Newark Free Library offer display cases to exhibit either individual or public organizations cultural interest, artifacts, or even a collection. These cases are meant to be used as a venue for the community and to enrich the library community in an educational manner. The Friends of the Newark Library committee review proposals for exhibits in the display cases, which are on a rotating exhibit schedule. My proposal was to exhibit a segment of the *Coupon Collection* as well as a summary of the statement for this collection. QR codes would accompany this statement and provide a visual of the alternating state between print and digital coupons.

I realized other aspects of the collecting process should be presented upon my proposal being accepted and preparation for the display. The archiving and management practice needed to be included. This not only supports the collection statement, but the concept of the collection process that was still in progress. The archiving information card for expiration month of June 2012 was presented with some of the June coupons. This was on it's own shelf within the display case. The display had its own signage acknowledging the use of the card and the ending tally for the month of June, which ended on the date of May 31, 2012. Since there was still a months time left for collecting June coupons, the public was given the information of the website address to have the option to continue to follow the *Coupon Collection* recent additions.

The opportunity to restage at a public institution offered the options for a diverse audience to view the collection in person and gave other individuals an opportunity to continue to view the collection via the *Collection Project* website. The *Coupon Collection* was on view from June 4 – August 17, 2012. I view the public display case as an intimate viewing space for the coupons and related materials to be presented. The display case was also approachable in the library's non-formal setting. I did not hear much feed back on how the collection was received by the library patrons. I was, however, invited back by the Friends of the Newark Free Library review committee to display another one of my artistic concepts.

The 2014 Mini Museum Group Exhibit was the site for my March restaging of the whole *Collection Project*. The exhibit ran from March 8th to April 5th, 2014 at the *It's All About Things* space in Port Chester, New York USA. For the March 2014 restaging of the *Collection Project*, an ephemeral print in the form of an 11" x 14" poster presented the current state of the collection. The posters displayed the web site address and QR code in the gallery space, which indicated the online existence of the *Collection Project*. I was offering the poster as a piece of memorabilia of the collection and the visitors to the gallery space had the option of obtaining the poster as a tangible object from the restaging.

These ephemeral concepts reference the art-historical shift of the dematerialization of art that occurred in the late 1960's. The dematerialization movement concerned placing the art creation materials into a secondary position and categorized the idea of art into a non-object form. My intention in investigating the dematerialization art theory is to find a way to present a tangible presence for my web-based artwork, rather than attempting to display the project by using a computer in the gallery space. The poster has elements of print media communication that I have designed for this specific moment in time of the March 2014 restaging of the collection.

The communication element was to promote the web-based art, the act of the continual collecting process, and to mobilize participants in the viewing process by allowing them to use their everyday digital devices. This was the second physical space that the whole collection was restaged in. The first site was curated as part of the Currents 2013 The Santa Fe International New Media Festival and was exhibited at a computer station at the festival site, El Museo Cultural de Santa Fe.

For this March 2014 restaging, I had an opportunity to present the project with complete artistic freedom. It is important to mention some of the background to how the *Collection Project* was chosen to be part of the group exhibit, along with arrangement for the presentation in the gallery space. It began with answering a call for proposals to the mini museum concept. The mini museum was approximately 14 in. x 10 in. x 13 in. represented an architectural model of a "white space" gallery. In my proposal, I perceived the mini museum as an object unto itself, since it had qualities of being an architectural model of a gallery space.

The restaging concept for my Internet-based collection investigated the dichotomy of space in which a collection is presented for public viewing. The two spaces I considered were a physical space in the museum and in cyberspace on a website. In my proposal, I stated that the mini museum is an object that visually represents a traditional form of where a specific collection is usually exhibited or stored. I intended to exhibit digital information in the form of visuals as a QR Code and Text for a website link in the mini museum space. In my proposal, these visuals would have presented the mini museum as a restaging site for digital media visual culture that would have acknowledged my "online" collection.

Even though my proposal did not get chosen for the site-specific mini museum, I was included in the accompanying group exhibition. This opportunity enabled me to consider some of my gallery presentation concepts with digital data in a different manner. In about a month's time before the mini museum exhibit opened, I corresponded and brain stormed with Luis Maldonado, the president and founder of *It's All About Things*.

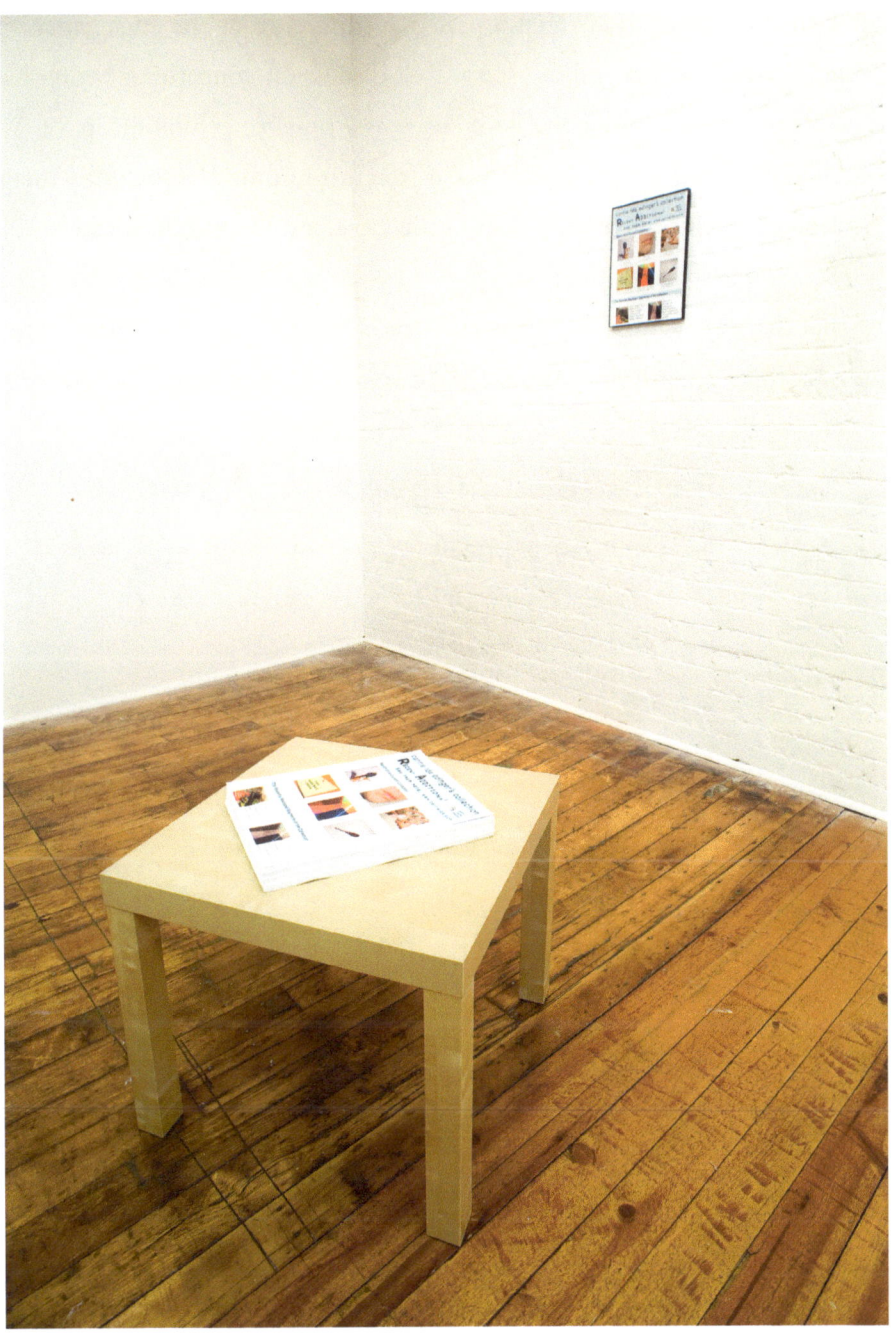

Fig.10. "Restaging" of the collection at It's All About Things space in Port Chester, NY
Image shows presentation of posters displayed at the experimental gallery space.

Our conversations covered topics that ranged from the engagement of digital devices in the gallery space to a discussion concerning which had more impact the wall or the floor space as a possible exhibition space. We both agreed to keep the presentation to a minimum. The included image was taken during the installation of the table and the posters in the *It's All About Things* space [Figure 10].

For the "restageing" of my Internet-based project, I chose the print media poster for its communication characteristics rather than fine art print

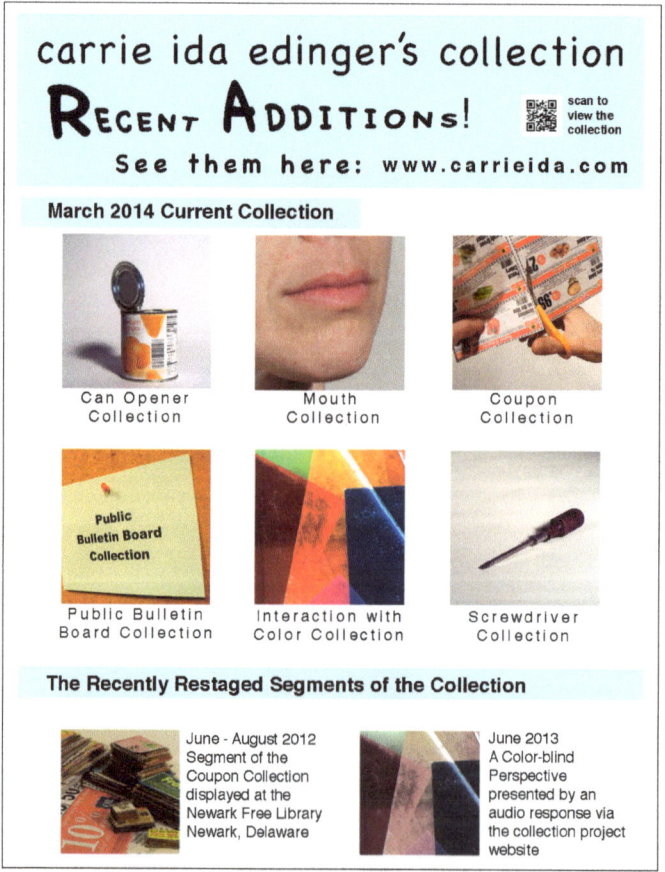

Fig.11. Print Media poster presenting the March 2014 state of the collection project. "Restaging" of the collection at It's All About Things space in Port Chester, NY Medium: laser/digitally printed, Poster Size: 11" x 14", Edition 250

aesthetics. My decision included the possibility that personal digital devices, such as smartphones, would mobilize participants in the viewing process of the Internet-based collection right in the gallery space. The gallery space did have Internet access, which can be seen as a motivational aspect for visitors to engage with their mobile devices and view an aspect of the collection. The "take away" concept of the poster is for viewers who do not have mobile devices and could have accessed the collection at another point in time [Figure 11]. I found it essential for me to access the gallery space for the "restaging" to complement both the physical and virtual spaces for a diverse audience to have accessibility and a sense of inclusiveness within the gallery space.

Both of these "restagings" involve the digital curation methods of maintaining and preserving a digital data lifecycle, which would be the digital objects that comprise the collection. In these "restagings," I also view the digital curation methods as a means to explore the concepts of engagement within both spaces of the exhibition. Both physical spaces of my "restagings," the library and the gallery, hosted an audience for the collection, but I needed to persuade them to become interested in my *Collection Project*. Methods of communication, such as the print media poster, are an important part of the curation process to acknowledge that the viewer needs to look beyond the physical spaces that house them to view the collection. Since, I was not physically there to observe each viewers actions, there is no cut and dry answer to confirm how many viewers participated with their digital devices to view the *Collection Project* website. My "restagings" and investigations about the physical and virtual spaces are not about factual statistic numbers of visitors. These curation methods concerning engagement are to inform the viewer that a collection can be presented in a non-object form.

TO COME FULL CIRCLE

The creative interest that spurred the idea for the last collection theme, *The Smell Collection*, was a moment from my presentation at the Ohio University School of Interdisciplinary Arts 50th anniversary conference in March of 2014. This presentation was during the early stages of research and my artistic practice for the *Collection Project*. The conference offered an intimate setting with a broad spectrum of peer perspectives and constructive dialog. Over the last three years of continued development with my *Collection Project*, I do reflect back to my peers input from that presentation entitled *Media & The Artist's Voice in Framing Interdisciplinary Practice*.

A video clip of myself blowing out a burning marshmallow on a stick then consuming it was the most memorable part of that specific presentation [Figure 12]. I played the video as I read the written text from the preliminary stages of my ethnography process to give an example of the details related to the common senses that I document.

SMELL – sweet, the sugar melting from the heat

TOUCH – warm from the mini fire burning the marshmallow

TASTE – warm and sweet with a carbon flavor from the melting/burning sugar

The comments and questions after the presentation revolved around this video clip. This moment gave me insight to how the visual and my text brought about so much inquiry. This ranged from how did you come about this inquiry to keep moving forward with this process. I knew the only thing that was missing from the video was the actual smell.

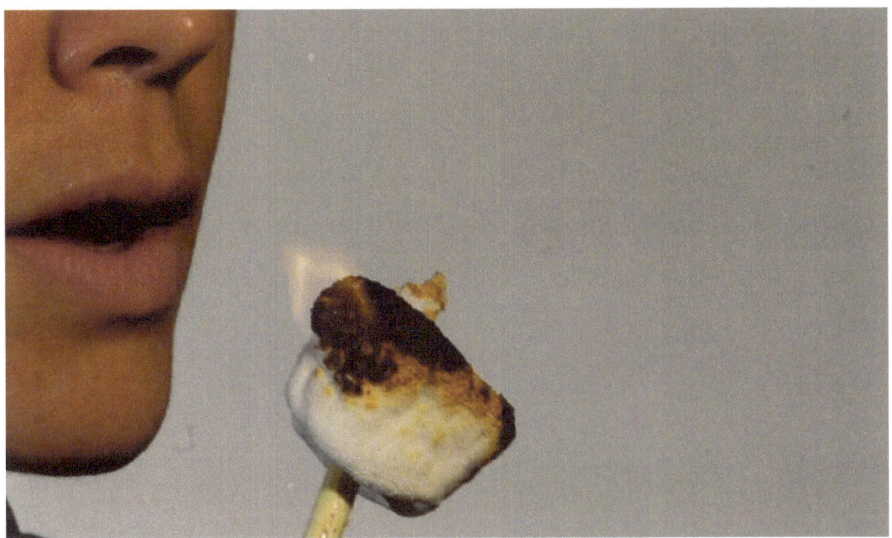

Fig.12. Still from June 2012 Video Clip blowing out a marshmallow on fire, from the Mouth Collection

The *Smell Collection* investigates the characteristics of video to acknowledge associations to specific aromas. Instead of the video clips presenting the functionality of the interaction between people and objects, the *Smell Collection* video clips are intended to facilitate recollections of individual experiences with the video representations of certain smells. Smells are still distinguished by individual emotional responses usually related to social bonding or experiences. The modern Western culture de-emphasized the sense of smell during the eighteenth and nineteenth centuries. This is with the comparison to primitive senses and the reference of animals. Smells are an aspect to the history of human culture by social hierarchies, gender, and social manners. The concepts of modernity placed the sense of sight as dominant during those centuries.

I do consider the *Smell Collection* to be more experimental than all the other collection themes. In my beginning research and development of methods for this collection, the conceptualization was dominated by audio and visual methods, which entailed questioning the utilization of the anthropological methods I borrowed to understand the social interaction between people and objects from the beginning stages of my *Collection Project*. I continued to investigate phenomenology, but from the art perspective. I considered the Fluxkits from the perspective of the participants experiencing the objects and events for themselves. The descriptions I read about the Fluxkits were the details from the multiscensory information that was notated from the activity of the Fluxkits and related events.

I was researching the Fluxkits as a personal inquiry of the senses. One specific FLuxkit the *Orifice Flux Plugs* by American Fluxus Artist, Larry Miller is linked to tactile experiences from the personal inquiry of the objects. The objects in this kit, such as a cork, were meant to examine scale, touch, and other sensory encounters. In focusing on the sense of smell as one of my collection themes, my research within the Fluxus movement led me to come across the *Smell Chess, Liquids* created by Fluxus artist, Takako Saito. I pursued my research beyond a textbook approach; even though the outcome had minimal results the experience led me back to my foundations with material culture.

As part of my research experience, I requested a viewing of the *Smell Chess, Liquids* at the Museum of Modern Art (MoMA) Department of Prints and Drawings Collection in New York City USA. In my request, I stated why it was necessary to view the object in person. I introduced the *Smell Collection* theme and how I was employing the characteristics of video to facilitate recollections associated with specific aromas to form this specific collection. I included with my description how objects from the Fluxus Movement offered the opportunity for participants to have a multisensory experience. An opportunity to observe the *Smell Chess,*

Liquids would have offered the ability to physically view an artwork from the 1960's, which is meant to be experienced in person and use the experience as a reference for my research with the human senses. I did also state that I had no intentions for the *Smell Chess, Liquids* to be included in the imagery/ video for my collection project, so it would be clear it was for art-based research purposes.

In my email correspondence with the MoMA staff from the Prints and Drawings Collection the *Smell Chess, Liquids* was unfortunately unavaible to be viewed, because it was stored off-site. The MoMA staff did offer to provide me with additional information about the object. Through our email exchange, I was provided with instructions from the *Sound Chess Set* made for John Cage by Takako Saito, but there was no documentation found about playing the *Smell Chess, Liquids* within the collection archive.

I was aware in sending my request that I would have no opportunity to touch the glass scent bottles that are the chess pieces. The *Smell Chess, Liquids* piece has become part of a museum collection and the object has gone through a transition from the original concept of personal engagement with the object to being archived with the intention of preservation. During that two or three week process, I felt that I have come full cycle with my reading of the *Fluxus Experience*. In the chapter, *Information and Experience*, there are details of how the act of sniffing was incorporated with the ritualized movement of the game of chess. This supplements the idea of text being significant to the ephemeral or participatory-based projects.

NEW MEDIA

AND

ENGAGEMENT

INTRODUCTION:
NEW MEDIA BEYOND AN ART MEDIUM

With my media research, I have crossed the disciplinary boundaries again into visual anthropology and museum studies. I found that visual practice was explored in a documentary manner and a hybrid format for fieldwork and presentations of projects within the anthropology discipline. From the museum studies perspective the Internet was considered as another space for viewers to experience the virtual form of museum culture. From both of these disciplines, I have taken away a parallel interest in utilizing media as a form of communication. Within the bigger cycle of research, it has brought me back to my own art discipline and specific media components, which have a foundation in mass communication.

As the art disciplines have progressed with technology and mass media, current new media art practices range from digital art to performance. My art practice has always been derived from some type of new media. My formal art education background began with printmaking and mediums that are related to women's labor, this is usually categorized as a craft or fiber arts. Even though these specific disciplines have been integrated into the fine art disciplines, they are part of the evolution of historical art movements from the traditional fine art disciplines of painting and sculpture. From investigating these art movements, I was able to explore how new media has been a means to represent social and cultural aspects within the art world.

Comparably to crossing the disciplinary boundaries, new media opens theory and practice beyond fine art concepts. The new media I am referring to is in the range of social media sites and as an agency for open communication. The communication aspect was important for the dissemination of my preliminary research for the *Collection Project*, along with the broader idea of presenting an artist's voice. I view these activities that are associated with this type of new media as part of my art practice. My art practice needs to be viewed from a perspective beyond the standard physical location of a studio. This perspective needs to be considered beyond the act of making objects. By perceiving new media beyond an art medium, I had the ability to include networked communication within my practice, which gave me the means to exchange information with an interdisciplinary audience.

A BLOG AS AN ARTIST'S WORKSPACE

The social media platform of a blog is an intangible workspace for self-publishing my developments of art-based research. I integrated blogging into my art practice as a means to publicly present preliminary digital sources and as a personal digital archiving agent. My blog examines the use of social media as a presentation platform and as a postmodern tool for developing knowledge that pertains to interdisciplinary practice.

My use of social media as a source for self-publishing preliminary artist-based research is in a continual process of reinterpretating knowledge. This process is derived from experiences and methods used with my current *Collection Project*. Artist and scholar, Graeme Sullivan's description for research practice is demonstrated with how artists in visual arts conceptualized their research. These approaches concerning the breath of the visual arts are centered toward the inquiry of the studio experience.

Sullivan argues the inquiry of the artist's experience encompasses ideas and the visuals that do inform individual, social, and cultural actions. Artist's daily social activities are included with these social and cultural actions, which are not bound by "studio" walls.

I wanted to expand the concept of my blog from its beginning stage, which was a promotional platform for my exhibitions and events pertaining to my art practice. Since the beginning stages, my blog has evolved in the first couple of years. Some of the writing stages included discussion of the material and developmental process of my artwork that lead to ideas toward the presentation of the artwork. These blog posts were lacking the presence of a wider source of research. I put aside writing about my art as an object and started to post about experiences in observing objects and the research I was engaged with while developing the *Collection Project*. Besides my subjective experience using the blog, the open access for the viewer of the blog is a source to explore wider resources, such as Internet links. Access to Internet links with my texts and images are regarded as obtainable information regarding the research for my collecting process and cross-discipline research.

Another artist and scholar, Margot Lovejoy refers to the tool types used by artists that tend to indicate the current technology conditions. The characteristics of the tools are integrated with the production and conceptualization of the artwork. The social media platform of a blog enables me to use various media tools to display my experiences and research. The significance for my self-publishing art-based research is the presentation of content, which contributes to the expanding cultural dialog that uses media and interdisciplinary practice within contemporary art.

The act of blogging supports the theory of production as presented by visual artist and artistic researcher Grete Refsum. The theory of production is based on the experiences or processes that occur before an artwork is finalized or even performed. My blog posts articulate the postmodern identities that are engaged in my art production process. In my research with the act of blogging, I came across scholar, Gill Kirkup's study with how the postmodern identity is based on how scholars use a blog to develop experiences and present multiple narratives with media. Kirkup presents in her academic blogging essay that there are concerns pertaining to the production of knowledge with this writing method. These concerns disseminate that the use of blogging does not follow the traditional peer review or editorial process of academic publications. The time honored publishing methods can alter the text from the original voice it was written in and may place in question views and experiences that can differ with gender, ethnicity, and a person's social economic class.

From Margot Lovejoy's research it is the tool types, which influence the artist's production and add context to the artwork. The tool and the technology conditions of the time period inform the production of art. Since the blog is a digital electronic tool and is based on programmed instructions, which automatically store, collect, transmit, and multiply visual and digital information. I use a pre-designed blog template to layout, transmit, and store my content. The blog is employed as an Internet source to present my experiences with methods and research for public access. The reinterpretation of knowledge from the experiences with my current *Collection Project* is developed with the act of the continual blogging process.

An example from my blog is a post about related research of my local newspaper's cutbacks in print editions. I wrote the post to understand the longevity of the collecting process involved in the *Coupon Collection*. The concept for the *Coupon Collection* is about the transition of the visual representation of the print media coupon form to a digital QR Code.

Referring back to Kirkup's concept of blogs forming a postmodern identity, the act of blogging allows me to describe my experiences in working with multiple narratives associated with the social research and the collaborations from the project. These multiple narratives represent the social and cultural actions that are occurring outside of my art practice.

Margot Lovejoy acknowledges in the first edition of her book, *Postmodern Currents*, the effect upon artists and their artwork with the use of technological tools is just beginning to be analyzed. With her analysis, she argues that it is important to consider aesthetic traditions and their role in technology use today. Lovejoy's argument is still important over twenty years later, with presently evolving digital media. Rather than focusing on the art history canon of conceptualism, and basing the theory that my blog is not valuing the Modernism ideals of an art object, I will examine a specific art historical collaboration between artists and engineers that Lovejoy uses as an example.

In the mid-1960's a new organization called "Experiments in Art and Technology" or E.A.T. was formed on a collaboration idea between artist and engineers. Artist, Robert Rauschenberg and scientist, Billy Kluver began E.A.T. on the concept of creating innovated work using technologies from that time frame. A large-scale project titled *Nine Evenings: Theater and Engineering* was established from the collaboration of thirty Bell Laboratory engineers, visual artists, dancers, and musicians. The 1966 project demonstrated that artists and engineers could collaborate.

Margot Lovejoy indicates that the collaboration had difficulties with each of the working styles of the artists and engineers toward the *Nine Evenings* performances. An example is coordinating engineers to finish technical support with theater deadlines in order for the artists to have ample time to rehearse. Lovejoy looks to specifics of the experiences from the project instead of resolving the problems. Two examples of her specifics where a longer amount of time to work on the project and the effort in which it is needed to contribute to the planning and scheduling of this style of performance. Lovejoy concludes her example with her perspective that both artists and engineers had to consider as well as learn new ways of thinking for the practical and the creative concepts that could interact with each other.

My experience with developing the structure of my blog evolved over a multiyear time frame. In this time period, I made a choice to change my ideas on writing a blog concerning my art practice and integrating interdisciplinary methods. A blog is a twenty-first century form of technology and is on a smaller scale than the *Nine Evenings* performances. I have had to learn new ways of thinking to present text and other media regarding the process of my art practice. Kirkup's reference to blogging as a scholarly product of "performative writing" implies the postmodern identity has a variety of narratives. These narratives produce a variety of roles in performance and presentation with a range of media.

From Kirkup's essay the academic professional engagement of blogging creates a new role for the academic identity. In addition, the theory can be identified alongside an artist's role in art-based research. Blogging offers public access to the varied processes that take place before an art concept is finalized. With this concept, I could refer back to the idea of new roles and how Sullivan implies that art practice has changed from being defined by an authoritative voice, such as that of aestheticians or art historians. Instead Sullivan argues the responsibilities are placed on the artist to be the cultural theorist and the practitioner. Construction of a theory of production is Grete Refsum's premise of how to establish a theoretical framework in the visual arts that Sullivan refers to. A theory of production concerns the happenings or processes before art is produce leading up to a finished project or an art object.

Both Refsum and Sullivan's arguments toward art practice imply a postmodern role for the artist, rather than a Modern concept of an artist in need of an outside authority source to distinguish the artist's process as well as the finished "art" object. Blogging has created a new role for text in my practice as an artist and scholar. I have utilized the social media platform of a blog to provide public accessibility to the theory of my production of process. Social media sites contribute to the growth of the network culture and placing the artists voice from a postmodern concept to having a link to global communication. A network culture extends the concepts of academic art terms that are placed on an artist's voice and text through the possibilities of digital culture and the immaterial production of information.

VIDEO AS RESEARCH

Video has two roles in my current *Collections Project*. The roles are as a digital object to form specific collection themes and as a form of visual research. The significance of video as research is to document my ethnographic roles in some part of the process of my fieldwork. One of my experiments included the use of the 60 second testimonial video format. I chose the specific time frame and the structuring of the video content for the corresponding presence it would have on the Internet. On my blog, I have included videos of myself as an artist employing the knowledge gained from my cross discipline process. These videos are intentionally produced with very short time frames, because of the context of the social media platform and the time period viewers engage with web content.

In my research with the background of video, I investigated the historical and theoretical aspects of video in regards to specific methods and the disciplines of art and anthropology. My inclusion of a brief synopsis from my readings is taken from the concepts of video art, visual anthropology, and experimental ethnography. Each of the individual readings presented the disciplines historical timeline with video that expanded the concepts of the traditional theories and specific methods from each discipline.

These three disciplines share the historical movement from the 1960's – 1980's of the technical side of video, which included the evolution of video camcorders to an affordable and portable format. Cinematic theories tend to be the foundation of the integration of video by the conceptual framework supporting film's relationship to reality and the production for the individual viewer. There was a time period for video to come into acceptance of use for each discipline. From the anthropology discipline, video in ethnography had to evolve and become accepted to represent knowledge. Video blurred the traditional fine art boundaries creating the mediums own language and references that move fine art mediums further away from the focus on specific media to how ideas are implemented.

Video is a multifaceted tool that integrates multiple narratives or identities along with conceptualization. I have considered these foundations with my continual pursuit of interdisciplinary practice through blogging and the process of my project. Referring back to Gill Kirkup's academic blogging essay, the blog format offers a presentation of the narrative of the self, but it provides a resource with various media to develop a postmodern identity. The act of blogging allows me to describe my experiences in working with multiple narratives associated with the social research and the collaborations for the project. I have had to consider new methods toward the presentation of text and other media. In this process there are opportunities between how the media and text support specific context. Video aids in the sensory investigation, but text makes a contribution to the theoretical elements. By acknowledging the human element role with blogging and the knowledge gained from multiple narratives, I can present these methods as potential development that relates to the breadth of theory and practice. My human experience and methodologies supplement the evolution of artists employing cross discipline methods.

Borrowing the 60 second video presentation continues my investigation with video as research. This method is derived from marketing concepts pertaining to the medium of video and the medium's ability to convey complex details with ease by a combination of sensory connections. The video production defines this style of communication as a short directed message pertaining to a product or specific identity of a person, which is similar to the concept of the elevator speech. My version of a *60 Second Testimonial* video format provides an example of my fieldwork ranging from my dual roles in my ethnography process to specific objects chosen for collection themes. The *Example of "fieldwork"* video is one of my first 60 second video presentations that was included on the July 27, 2013 blog post. Looking back on this video, I see my progress with being able to articulate my process with borrowed methods, while visually presenting the roles within the process.

At least four years have passed since I shot this video. Since I have not viewed the video in sometime, I noticed the setting for the video was sparse and had a makeshift environment. I have captured the same style from my videos that formed my collection themes. By presenting my practice in a stark environment, I have been able to direct the viewer's focus to my collecting process. The video is also very direct with its content, which was the objective of borrowing the 60 second format. The documentation concerning the text with the process could have had some other visual details. This would of given the viewer more insight to why text is important in the preliminary fieldwork process.

Approximately two years later, a participant of the collection project agreed to contribute to the video as research. A single video clip represents the addition to the March 2015 *Mouth Collection*, which focused on sound with the genre of music hip-hop or rapping. Bill Ferrell a.k.a. Gentle Jones is a local rapper in my Mid-Atlantic region of the US. He contributed his original A capella vocals. For the video as research my inquiry was about Gentle Jones' embodied experience with rapping and creating sound. Instead of doing a traditional question and answer format, I emailed my points of inquiry prior to our meeting for producing the video clip. I wanted him to consider his response and personal experiences.

MY POINTS OF INQUIRY:

- when using his vocals could he explain the motion or activity of his mouth?

- could he go into detail about the connection with the beat of the music and his vocals?

- when he is rapping could he describe his overall experience?

In my conversation with Gentle Jones about the overall content for his video clip, I was referring to his activity and that it did not involve another object – as in the activity of creating sound with his body. Gentle Jones shared his perspective with me that the object was the audience. While working through the process of editing the video and audio, I thought about our conversation. In the video as research, Gentle Jones describes that he is aware of the audience in the room with him and "between us all it is magic." The audience is consuming Gentle Jones' vocals through the enjoyment of audio entertainment. This not only includes another perception to the collection, but to include how the element of sound expands the description of the dual functionality of the *Mouth Collection*, which has been focused on individual consumption.

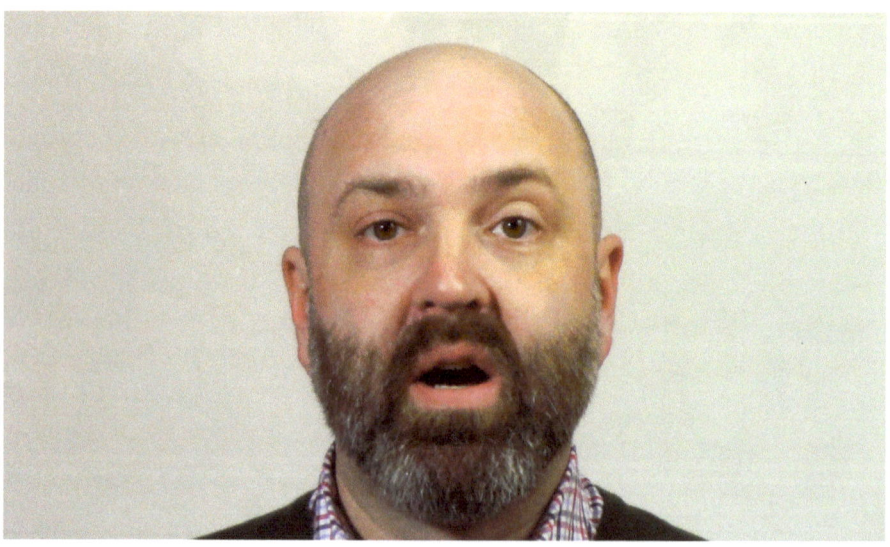

Fig.13. Still from March 2015 Video Clip video as research with Bill Ferrell a.k.a. Gentle Jones, from the Mouth Collection

A technical element of the video as research with Gentle Jones is that it was overdubbed on the video clip that was included in the *Mouth Collection*. The framing for the *Mouth Collection* had a focus for the majority of the collecting process on a close-up of the mouth area. I selected a frontal pose for framing this video clip [Figure 13]. This is to present a focus on his facial expressions in conjunction with the mouth movements. I modified the video to play in half its original speed. This slows down Gentle Jones' motion just enough to bring notice to the detail of the facial expressions, while excluding the original audio from the collections clip. This specific video as research had the same short time-frame, but the content was conceptualized with several layers instead of the direct approach of my first 60 second video.

Both of these examples of video as research depict the duality of theory and practice of my *Collection Project*. The videos present the project's foundation with my personal investigations and a collaborative element, which contributes a different viewpoint toward the *Mouth Collection*. These videos as research are meant to expand both the disciplines of art and anthropology standards of video as representation. While I have utilized a video format to present the content in a shorter time frame and performed selective editing, these videos do demonstrated video as a multifaceted tool that integrates multiple narratives or identities along with conceptualization. This integration not only represents interdisciplinary practice, but also the many layered gray areas in my research concerning the process of interdisciplinary methods.

SOCIAL MEDIA AND PUBLIC ACCESSIBILITY

The inclusion of social media links on the *Collection Project's* website offered the opportunity for viewers to follow the collection's progress. In addition, I viewed the social media links as part of my investigation of the public accessibility to my collection. I was examining how digital links had the possibilities to extend concepts related to public space for viewing a collecting process. As my time progressed in posting information about the collection's progress on selected social media sites, I came to a realization that the network culture elements were minimized with some social media sites and the corporate culture became the focus of my research and experiences.

I used three different Internet platforms for my project. A website presented the *Collection Project* and a blog presented the background of my practice. I posted on various social media sites to provide accessibility to the updated information pertaining to the collection. Through digital links from other social media sites the viewers could share or view a portion of my collection. During the duration of the project, I most frequently posted on the social media sites of Google + and Facebook. I included links on the main *Collection Project* website from these two social media sites. Both of these sites were utilized in the initial stages of the project while the specific social media sites attracted a following to the project.

I will refer to Facebook as an example from my social media experiences and the absences with public availability of my posts. A 2012 change in the Facebook fan page policy has made me inquire about the future use of this style of social media site. These changes concerned prioritizing those pages that have the most activity or "Likes." This began to alter the Facebook news feed of posts and status of the fan webpage. At the end of May 2012, Facebook launched a "pay to promote post" policy to reach a greater percentage of the fans following a page. My Facebook collection's page was in the initial stages of developing a following. I had no intentions of paying for marketing promotions for my *Collection Project*, since the social networking page was intended to promote an online social interaction with the recent additions posted on my main website. I was interested in the actual public accessibility to the *Collection Project*'s recent additions through the network culture context and not by the social media site as a brand-marketing tool.

In my online research there was an article from Adweek, which states that Facebook is offering a "Pages Only" News Feed that will post the pages a user only has "Liked." This is after Facebook responded to their member's request that they want to see the pages from all the fan pages they were connected with. This does not insure that all posts from fan pages will be seen. That is still a matter of uncertainty, which is dependant on how many fan pages the user is following and the number of post by those fan pages per day. I could acknowledge that there were subtle changes occurring and Facebook altered its features for testing new marketing strategies.

During my experience and research of posting on the Facebook fan page, my investigation has been focused on public access for those who are not Facebook members. The Facebook fan page can be seen on the Internet without logging into the Facebook site, but there are absences in what content is publicly available. The page cannot be interacted with; for example, I use the "ask a question" feature in correspondence with my recent addition postings. This information is accessible and stored within the Facebook online structure. The other information that is within the structure is the responses to the posts. The history of those responses cannot be seen without logging into the site. As my page went through a brief development it would have been convenient if it had full public access for those viewers who are interested in using the information available for future media or even material culture research.

The inventor of the World Wide Web, Tim Berners-Lee references the Internet's initial concept was to have universality. Social media sites and search engines have evolved to the threatening concepts of being central platforms on the Internet. Berners-Lee refers to these types of sites as silos of information on the web, but the data is not accessible or easily transferable to another site. It is common knowledge that Facebook has this type of presence on the web. My continual use of Facebook through 2013 brought features that were no longer available and features that I could not activate, because I did not have more than 100 "likes" for the collections fan page.

In 2014 my Facebook experience consisted of their marketing strategy to purchase their online ads. The cycle of Facebook's ad sale campaign did alter my page manager screen with many types of "advertise your page" buttons and notifications. In addition, these notifications sporadically interrupted my direct login to the page and lead me to Facebook ad information. The collection fan page became a nonfunctional social media site unless I bought a Facebook ad. One notification that interrupted my directed login reminded me of making efforts to meet a quota of "Likes."

This made me decide to no longer post on the page. I did not delete the collections fan page. Instead the Facebook page has become part of the social media research toward the interdisciplinary aspect of my project. The intent of this specific example is not to slander a major social media site, but is toward research for the Internet-based *Collection Project*. The social media research element is utilized to investigate social media sites as links to digital media art and exploring the context of public accessibility by means of a virtual space.

The visual is my social media connection analysis [Figure 14], which is based on the two-year investigation with the social network links for the Internet-based *Collection Project*. The investigations began with two popular social media sites, Goggle+ and Facebook. The analysis includes my blog, since that specific hyperlink provided public access to my experiences and research in forming the collection. The experimental process from the 2013 *Public Bulletin Board Collection* theme is also presented with the two stages of a public collecting process. This connection analysis is not based on statistics that pertain to the daily hits on my website or "likes" on my Facebook Fan Page. It is based on the engagement of a specific social media site and is concerned from the posts of a period of time.

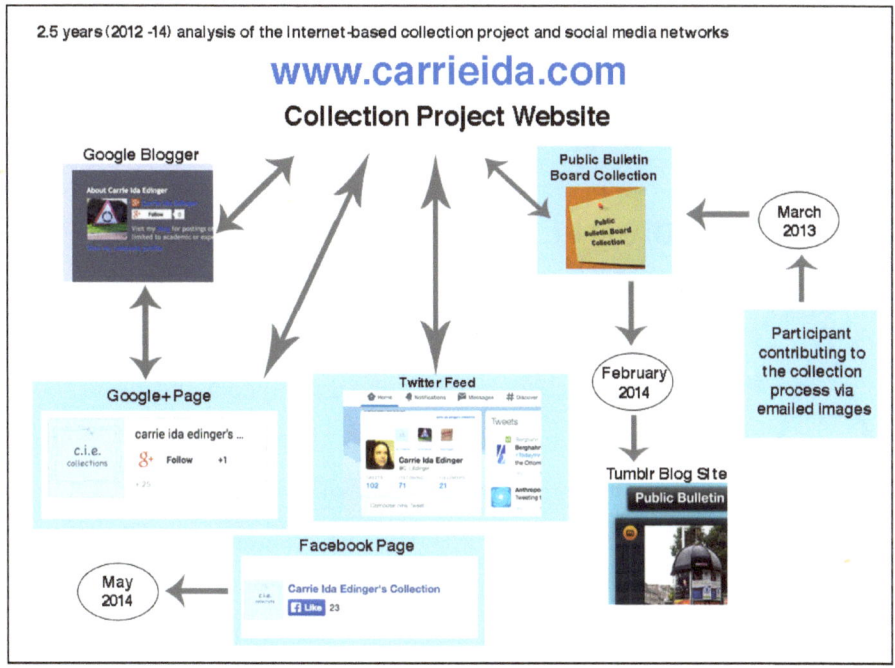

Fig.14. Social media connection analysis from May 30, 2014 Blog Post, Digital Creation Date: 2014

My connection analysis visually presents the connection to the main collection project website. I kept to my original guidelines of maintaining the project's content on one site. This is similar to the idea of a physical space of a museum housing a collection. Referring back to my original inquiry concerning the public accessibility of digital links to my collection and from my related social media research, I have come to the conclusion that various opportunities from physical and virtual social spaces are needed in order to have the ability to "link" people to a project with an Internet-based platform. From my participation with a couple of social media sites, I have realized they have limited results as a source for public accessibility. My reasoning comes from my engagement with my "restagings" of the *Collection Project* in experimental spaces and my research with the constant changes occurring with corporate strategies and features of social media sites.

THE DIGITAL AND SOCIAL OF NET.ART

As my collection project has evolved over a four-year period, I have investigated the characteristics of digital media and related social aesthetics to form these collection themes. I wanted to define the term social, since it has its own breadth within contemporary art. I am investigating the human experience with the dichotomy of space. The two spaces I am referring to are our physical space and cyberspace, which are both examined in my collecting process and public accessibility of the collection.

An example from the collection that employs a social media site as part of the collecting process is the *Public Bulletin Board Collection*. The *Public Bulletin Board Collection* theme is formed from my observations of the transition from print media to digital and the public access to communication or the network systems. This collection theme is investigating physical environments and if public bulletin boards are still being maintained within various communities.

Public bulletin boards are a physical social space to communicate information concerning events and opportunities in a community. For my Internet-based *Public Bulletin Board Collection* I use a social media site to archive images of these physical spaces that are still in use for community communication. The focus of the collecting process is based upon participation from the public, which is to submit digital images of a public bulletin board in a participants residing community.

The first method used in the collecting process was with email for participants to submit images. This is with the intention to post the images on the collection project main website. A year into this theme and with sparse submissions, I relocated the collection to a Tumblr blog site [Figure 15]. The Tumblr blog site as a public interactive site offers an option of allowing people to submit posts with various media, such as images, text, and links. Participants posting these types of digital media were intended to contribute individually to the digital collecting process of this collection theme.

A hybrid approach is explored through the collecting process by means of contemporary social practice and the interactive components of the social media site, Tumblr. Three motivational concepts are proposed by art historian and critic Claire Bishop that have been used since the 1960's to encourage participation in an art related social experience. They are activation, authorship, and community. I will introduce Bishop's three motivational concepts with the collecting process from the physical space, which is the site of the public bulletin board to the Tumblr social media site.

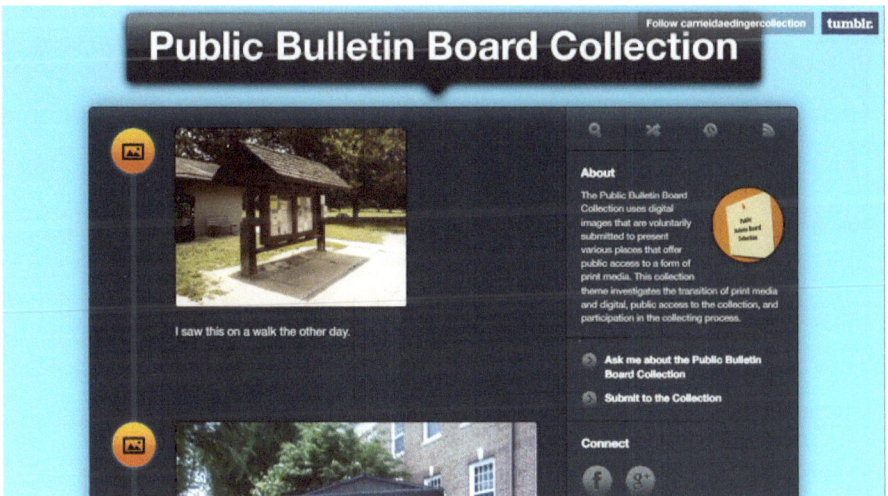

Fig.15. Screenshot of a portion of the Public Bulletin Board Collection Tumblr site. Source: carrieidaedingercollection.tumblr.com last modified 2015.

Activation is defined as the creation of an active subject matter, along with offering the participant an experience of physical or symbolic participation. The interaction between the participant in the physical space and various forms of digital media supply the agency or performative element to contribute to the *Public Bulletin Board Collection*. The intention was for participants to post image-based content with their hand held digital devices. My objective of the *Public Bulletin Board Collection* was to mobilize participants with their everyday digital devices in the collecting process.

The second motivational aspect is authorship. The Tumblr site offers an opportunity for public contributions to be included to the collection theme. The public contribution references back to the opportunity of engagement by the online viewers or participants forming a multi-voice effect for the collection to be formed. Each individual post on the Tumblr site is an activity that is parallel to Bishop's authorship context with a democratic agenda, but it also broadens the context by reaching beyond a finished project that has the opportunity to continue by the malleable characteristics of the Internet and the Tumblr blog site remaining open to the public.

As for community, the collection theme is about utilizing a social media site to archive images of these physical spaces still in use for community communication. In Bishop's argument she is skeptical toward the collective dimension of the social experience and ephemeral projects. This is referenced with her inquiry to individual and collective agency, along with how the documentation of social practice is presented for the future use of these projects. I view the interactive components and continuous open access of the Tumblr site as a shift in the context of the 1960's social experience of participatory art.

The social media's interactive components offer the opportunity for participants to post at any given time. Even if the Tumblr site is dormant for over a year, a post from a participant can revitalize the site. This virtual space has the opposite context of the 1960's social experience by not having a limited timeframe for participation that a physical site conveys. Considering the Tumblr site beyond a singular collection theme of the *Public Bulletin Board Collection*, social media was a source for public access to the continuous collecting process of this collection.

I have evaluated this collection theme by asking why would it be important to participate in this collecting process. The question led to other inquires pertaining to the sparseness of social engagement and public awareness with the activity that was needed for the collecting process. I do not categorize these inquiries within my project as failures. With my own experience's related to my art practice and research, I view this reflective process to understand the missing entity within the project structure. This part of the progress can be related to the old adage of learning from previous experiences. The main structure of the social engagement can be implemented in another type of project or collaboration.

My choice of this social media site was to create awareness of this collection theme, but limiting the engagement through cyberspace hindered this type of activity that was needed. This collecting process needed some kind of simultaneous connection happening virtually and at a physical space. I have presented this collection theme at a physical space, which was a panel session at the 2016 College Art Association Conference. This was a formal academic presentation about the theoretical background of the conceptualization of the project. Through these experiences, I have determined what is needed is a physical event with a possible captive audience that can be motivated to participate in the collecting process with their digital devices. As for the theme of the *Public Bulletin Board Collection*, I can attest that the theme is derived from my own personal interest with the transition of print and digital communication. As a future direction with a public collecting process a broader theme or even focusing on a specificity of a local identity would create more of a direct interest that could lead to participation.

CONCLUSION:
AN ARTIST'S RESPONSE TO "CRITICISM"

O f course, there will always be some kind of criticism even when the idea of being an art critic is no longer in vogue. My conclusion is edited from an earlier essay I wrote for a submission to an online art research journal that had a call for a criticism theme. My original essay was written in a more formal academic format and my argument was not in favor of American Art Critic and Historian, Hal Foster's theory of what he has termed "quasi-anthropological" use of ethnography in contemporary art.

During the time frame of Foster's essay the integration of digital media, especially the Internet, with contemporary projects where at their beginning stages. Digital media offers the opportunity to have another platform of public presentation for a continual critical study, while extending various modes of engagement and communication to project concepts. In my initial stages of research from specific 1990's art criticism essays, my over all analysis from my reading is that the 1990's stereotypes that are derived from those essays need to be set aside to further the knowledge of interdisciplinary practice.

My investigation of an art criticism text, *The Artist as Ethnographer*, offered the examination of methodological approaches with the concept of borrowing another discipline's methods such as ethnography. Hal Foster wrote this specific essay. He cites the grand narratives of Walter Benjamin and Marxism, while these theories are relevant to the understanding of the role of the artist to authorship and the concepts of social classes within the art world; I was investigating examples of artists engaging with ethnography as a process, the roles within research and specific projects.

These specific themes were sparse in his two versions of the essays published approximately a year apart.

The 1995 edited version was published in the book, *The Traffic in Culture Refiguring Art and Anthropology*. A year later, Foster published a longer version of the essay in his book, *The Return of the Real*. Both essays refer to the collaboration between artist and art institutions with site-specific projects and the inclusion of the theory of the "ethnographic turn" between art and anthropology.

Foster has focused on the formulation from the collaboration between an art institution as the sponsor and the artist, but from his examples there were minimal insightful details concerning the methods employed in the ethnographic process leading to an exhibition or completed project. He regards the majority of these site-specific projects resulting in an investigation of "ethnographic self-fashioning." If Foster had included detailed examples from the artist perspective of methods, I believe this would have enabled his critique to be more comprehensive rather than his descriptive criticism label of a typical "quasi-anthropological" scenario outcome.

Foster has categorized autoethnography as his number two problem with "quasi-anthropological" art. He has quite a few terms to describe the process, such as self-othering, pseudoethnographic reports in art, and the practice of philosophical narcissism. Foster's art historian and critic perspective of an artist's approach with cross-discipline methods refers back to my introduction and Dr. Kristine Stiles argument that concerns who has the authoritarian voice between art critic/ historian and artist. This dual role as artist researcher allows the ability to analyze a practice-base inquiry. The practitioner researcher and scholar as an author shifts the perspective of the work of art as a product from the art criticism context to the production of knowledge from a critical discourse of a practice-led inquiry.

While Foster has coined terms for the dangers of the reflexivity in these enthographic positions, I do consider my approach to reach beyond Foster's theory of a confessional testimony. Currently in my research, I have not discovered an ample amount of published texts by artists referring to their ethnography process or related research for a specific interdisciplinary project. My investigations toward autoethnography or considering the various roles in the ethnography process have been considered from the Anthropology discipline.

The introduction of reflexivity in ethnography enabled subjective experiences to be included within the research process. This is also known in the ethnographic process as a tool in fieldwork or the empathic approach. This method changed the ethnographical objective documentation by unifying the "natives" or marginalized person's experience with subjective methods. While the anthropology discipline has its own debate over the quality of data and the ethnographic truth derived from these subjective methods, there is an important position that self-reflexivity can aid in the production of knowledge.

Published in the same decade as Foster, Judith Okely and Helen Callaway published a collection of autobiographical essays, which inquires about the notions and contributions from anthropologist's fieldwork in this style of written text. Okely and Callaway examine the narcissism label when reflexivity is an element of an anthropologist's text. Their argument is based around the fundamental aspect of how relationships are established by a cross-cultural encounter within fieldwork. They refer to a classical Greek myth as an example to the difference between self-adoration and self-awareness. They define the difference between self-adoration and self-awareness in how the self is positioned within the autobiography. A writing style that protects the self from critical study and does not take into consideration any of the problematic relations between the presence and background of the fieldworker and others in the field is not befitting from reflexivity.

My intention for forming my Internet-based collection project was to employ these ethnographic methods to establish various viewpoints to be considered. The importance of my position within this text is that borrowing the self-reflexivity method has been productive to the knowledge that has formed my ephemeral collection. In my use of the ethnography process, I have developed methods toward theory and practice that persuade me to not acknowledge Foster's dangers using reflexivity from an art criticism perspective.

I do not agree with Foster's argument toward ethnographer envy among artists. I did not venture into interdisciplinary practice, because of Foster's descriptions of one discipline using another's methods for competitive gain. My interest was in representing everyday objects from American Western Culture beyond the conventional visual representation of the fine art discipline and museum environment. However, I do agree with Foster's views about the time allocated to implement a project. I could relate to his argument with a short time-period that puts into question the impact on the engagement with an artist and a community group. My views come from my experiences as a visiting artist with art institutions and community centers. Sometimes I did leave a finished project and wondered what the outcome would have been if we had more time together with the specific group of people involved with a project.

In Foster's 1995 edited essay, he refers to the length of time given toward projects and the inability to establish relationships between a community and an artist. As Foster describes the artist engagement with the collaboration, he refers to how there is little time or money for a quality allotted period of time to be able to interact with the community. In his scenario, Foster argues that a minimal amount of time given for a project causes limited engagement with all aspects of the collaboration and this is what determines his theory of "ethnographic self-fashioning." Since my Internet-based project is an independent project, I have chosen to spend a significant amount of time with the project and pertaining research. This is not intended to appease Foster's argument of the lack of interaction with the community, but to develop and analyze the borrowed methods used toward my project. Within a four-year time period the development of specific methods has been achieved by utilizing social media as a network link to each monthly addition of collection themes and my preliminary research.

These digital modes alter the traditional concepts of critical theory to allow a platform that provides the opportunity of including multiple voices. Of course, my response to criticism is in favor of the integration of an artist's voice as part of the construction of research methodologies as well as defining how social and cultural implications develop their concepts. I did not write this text with a narcissistic artist agenda, but to contribute to the gaps of cross discipline approaches within the humanities.

REFERENCES

Introduction: The Absence of the Artist's Voice

Abu-Lughod, Lilia. 1993. *Writing Women's Worlds*. Berkeley, University of California Press.

Abu-Lughod, Lila. 1991. "Writing Against Culture," in *Recapturing Anthropology*, edited by Richard G. Fox, 137–162 Santa Fe, School of American Research Press.

Barrett, Estelle and Bolt, Barbara eds. 2007. *Practice as Research Approaches to Creative Arts Enquiry*. London, I.B. Tauris & Co. LTD.

Pink, Sarah. 2009. *Doing Sensory Ethnography*. London, SAGE Publications Inc.

Piper, Adrian. 1996. *Out of Order, Out of Sight Volume 1: Selected Writings in Meta-Art 1968 – 1992*. Cambridge: The MIT Press.

Piper, Adrian. 1996. *Out of Order, Out of Sight Volume 2: Selected Writings in Art Criticism 1967 - 1992*. Cambridge: The MIT Press.

Sansi, Roger. 2015. *Art, Anthropology and the Gift*. London, Bloomsbury.

Schneider, Arnd and Wright, Christopher eds. 2006. *Contemporary Art and Anthropology*. London, Bloomsbury.

Schneider, Arnd and Wright, Christopher eds. 2010. *Between Art and Anthropology*. London, Bloomsbury.

Schneider, Arnd and Wright, Christopher eds. 2013. *Anthropology and Art Practice*. London, Bloomsbury.

Seidman Stephen. 1994. *The Postmodern Turn New Perspectives on Social Theory*. Cambridge, Cambridge University Press.

Stiles, Kristine. 1996. "General Introduction," in *Theories and Documents of Contemporary Art A Sourcebook of Artists' Writings*, edited by Kristine Stiles and Peter Selz, 1–9. Berkeley: University of California Press.

ART AND ANTHROPOLOGY

The Artist's Positionality

Edinger, Carrie. 2011. *Transformation of Personhood Through the Concept of Work*. Master of Arts Thesis, Edinburgh College of Art, University of Edinburgh of Scotland.

Kosuth, Joseph. 1991. *Art After Philosophy and After*. edited by G. Guercio, Cambridge, The MIT Press.

Marx, Jerry D. 2011. "American social policy in the Great Depression and World War II." Accessed April 12, 2016. socialwelfare.library.vcu.edu/eras/greatdepression/american-social-policy-in-the-great-depression-and-wwii/.

Okely, Judith. 2012. "Confronting Positionality," in *Teaching Anthropology*. Vol. 2, no.1, pp. 36-43.

Sullivan, Graeme. 2005. *Art Practice as Research*. London, Sage Publications.

Beginning the Ethnographic Process with Text

Coffey, Amanda. 1999. *The Ethnographic Self Fieldwork and the Representation of Identity*. London, Sage Publications.

Edinger, Carrie. 2013. "Video Research And Interdisciplinary." Accessed April 10, 2013. carrieidaedinger.blogspot.com/2013/04/video-research-and-interdisciplinary.html.

Edinger, Carrie. 2015. "MouthClip Outtakes and Reflections." Accessed January 12, 2014. carrieidaedinger.blogspot.com/2014/01/mouth-clip-outtakes-and-reflections.html.

Pink, Sarah. 2009. *Doing Sensory Ethnography*. London, SAGE Publications Inc.

Russell, Catherine. 1999. *Experimental Ethnography*. Durham, Duke University Press.

Borrowing Methods and Ethnographic Roles

Coffey, Amanda. 1999. *The Ethnographic Self Fieldwork and the Representation of Identity*. London, Sage Publications.

Goldberg, RoseLee. 1988. *Performance Art From Futurism to the Present*. New York, Harry N. Abrams Inc.

Perlman, Helen Harris. 1968. *Persona Social Role and Personality*. Chicago, University of Chicago Press.

Weber, Robert. 2000. The Created Self. New York, W.W. Norton & Company.

Carrie Ida Edinger's official website. "Carrie Ida Edinger's Collections." Last modified June 2018. carrieida.com/Collections.html.

Edinger, Carrie. 2012. "Roles within Enthnography Stages." Accessed July 30, 2012. carrieidaedinger.blogspot.com/2012/07/roles-within-ethnography-stages.html.

Edinger, Carrie. 2013. "Ethnographic Roles." Accessed March 7, 2013. carrieidaedinger. blogspot.com/2013/03/ethnographic-roles.html.

The Lived Experience and The Collection

Lindsay, Shawn. 1996. "Hand Drumming." in *Things as They Are New Directions in Phenomenological Anthropology*, edited by Michael Jackson, 196–212. Bloomington, Indiana University Press.

Pinney, Christopher. 2006. "Four Types of Visual Culture," in *Handbook of Material Culture*, edited by Chris Tilley, et al. 131–144. London, Sage Publication.

Ram, K.Kalpana and Houston, Christopher eds. 2015. *Phenomenology in Anthropology A Sense of Perspective*. Bloomington, Indiana University Press.

Edinger, Carrie. 2012. "Transformation of a Proposal." Accessed April 25, 2012. carrieidaedinger.blogspot.com/2012/04/transformation-of-proposal.html.

"We Are Colorblind." 2012. Accessed May 28, 2013. color-blindness.com/2009/01/06/50-facts-about-color-blindness/.

"We Are Colorblind." 2012. Accessed: May 28, 2013. wearecolorblind.com/article/a-quick-introduction-to-color-blindness/.

Art and Anthropology with Agency

Fox, Richard ed. 1991. *Recapturing Anthropology.* Santa Fe, School of American Research Press.

Gell, Alfred. 1998. *Art and Agency.* Oxford, Clarendon Press.

Goggin, Maureen Daly and Tobin, Beth Fowkes eds. 2009. *Women and Things, 1750 – 1950.* Surrey UK, Ashgate Publishing Limited.

Grimshaw, Anna and Ravetz, Amanda eds. 2005. *Visualizing Anthropology.* Bristol, Intellect Books.

Heller, Roanna. 2005. "Becoming an Artist-Ethnographer". in *Visualizing Anthropology,* edited by Anna Grimshaw and Amanda Ravetz, 133–142. Bristol, Intellect Books.

Ingold, Tim. 2013. *Making Anthropology, Archaeology, Art and Architecture.* London, Routledge.

Klein, Julie Thompson. 1996. *Crossing Boundaries Knowledge, Disciplinarities, and Interdisciplinarities.* Charlottesville, University Press of Virginia.

Klein, Julie Thompson. 1996. *Interdisciplinarity History, Theory, and Practice.* Detroit, Wayne State University Press.

Kouritzin, Sandra, et al. 2009. *Qualitative Research Challenging the Orthodoxies in Standard Academic Discourse(s).* New York, Routledge.

Leavy, Patricia. 2009. *Method Meets Art Arts-Based Research Practice.* New York, The Guilford Press.

REDEFINING AN EPHEMERAL COLLECTION

Introduction: The Collection and The Internet

Varnelis, Kazys. 2010. "The meaning of network culture (1)." openDemocracy. Accessed December 26, 2016. opendemocracy.net/kazys-varnelis/meaning-of-network-culture-1.

Cantor, Jay. 1985. *Winterthur.* New York, Abrams.

Burnett, Robert, et al. 2011. *The Handbook of Internet Studies.* Oxford, Wiley-Blackwell.

Goriunova, Olga. 2012. *Art Platforms and Cultural Production on the Internet.* New York, Routledge.

Graham, Beryl, et al. 2010. *Rethinking Curating: art after new media.* Cambridge, MIT Press.

Graham, Beryl. ed. 2014. *New Collecting: exhibiting and audiences after new media art.* Surrey, England; Ashgate.

Moist, Kevin and Banash, David eds. 2013. *Contemporary Collecting Objects, Practices, and the Fate of Things.* Plymouth UK, Scarecrow Press, Inc.

Rinehart, Richard and Ippolito, Jon. 2014. *Re-collection Art, New Media, and Social Memory.* Cambridge, The MIT Press.

Strasser, Susan. 1999. *Waste and Want A Social History of Trash.* New York, Owl Books Henry Holt and Company.

Tsatsou, Panayiota. 2014. *Internet Studies Past, Present and Future Directions.* Surrey. Ashgate Publishing Limited.

Yokota, Kariann Akemi. 2011. *Unbecoming British: how revolutionary America became a postcolonial nation*. Oxford, Oxford University Press.

Transition of Media

Bauer, Alexander and Agbe-Davies, Anna eds. 2010. *Social Archaeologies of Trade and Exchange*. Walnut Creek, Left Coast Press.

Edinger, Carrie. 2012. "Print Media Coupon as Artifact." Accessed Spring of 2012. carrieida.com/CouponCollection.html.

Miller, Daniel. 1987. *Material Culture and Mass Consumption*. Oxford, Basil Blackwell.

Pearce, Susan. 1990 *Archaeological Curatorship*. London, Leicester University Press.

Rubin, C. 2010. "Coupon Use Hits Record Highs." New York City, Inc. Accessed Dec. 2, 2011. inc.com/topic/inmar%20inc.

Tuttle, B. 2010. "The History of Coupons." Time Moneyland. Accessed Dec. 2, 2011. articles. moneycentral.msn.com/SavingandDebt/SaveMoney/TheDeathOfTheCoupon.aspx?page=1.

The Everyday and Redefining Material Culture

Daly Goggin, M. and Fowkes Tobin, B. 2009. *Women and Things, 1750-1950*. Surrey, Ashgate Publishing Limited.

Edinger, Carrie. 2011. *Transformation of Personhood Through the Concept of Work*. Master of Arts Thesis, Edinburgh College of Art, University of Edinburgh of Scotland.

Hoskins, Janet. 1998. *Biographical Objects How Things Tell the Stories of People's Lives*. New York, Routledge.

Knappett, Carl. 2005. *Thinking Through Material Culture*. Philadelphia, University of Pennsylvania Press.

Leavy, Patricia. 2009. *Method Meets Art Arts-Based Research Practice*. New York, The Guilford Press.

Strasser, Susan. 1999. *Waste and Want A Social History of Trash*. New York, Owl Books Henry Holt and Company.

"Restaging" in the Physical and Virtual Space

Mallonee, Laura. 2014. "Why Are There So Many Art Exhibition Revivals?" Accessed May 28, 2016. hyperallergic.com/138834/why-are-there-so-many-art-exhibition-revivals/.

The Digital Curation Centre (DCC) official website. "What is digital curation." Accessed September 18, 2016. dcc.ac.uk/digital-curation/what-digital-curation.

Bishop, Claire. 2006. *Participation*. London, Whitechapel.

Bishop, Claire. 2014. *Radical Museology*. London, Koenig.

Graham, Beryl. ed. 2014. *New Collecting: exhibiting and audiences after new media art.* Surrey, England; Ashgate.

Kwon, Miwon. 2003. "Exchange Rate: An Obligation and Reciprocity in Some Art of the 1960's and After." in *Work Ethic*, Helen Molesworth, University Park, Pennsylvania State University Press.

Lippard, Lucy. 1973. *Six Years: the dematerialization of the art object from 1966 to 1972...* Berkeley, University of California Press.

Rinehart, Richard and Ippolito, Jon. 2014. *Re-collection Art, New Media, and Social Memory.* Cambridge, The MIT Press.

To Come Full Circle

Classen, Constance, et al. 1994. *Aroma The Cultural History of Smell.* London; Routledge.

Higgins, Hannah. 2002. *Fluxus Experience.* Berkely, University of California.

"retrospectives & future visions." Ohio University, School of Interdisciplinary Arts, Athens, Ohio Accessed: March 20, 2014. ohio.edu/finearts/upload/InterArts_con_program_3-10-14.pdf.

Saito, Takako. 1965. "Smell Chess, Liquids." New York, Museum of Modern Art Accessed: April 28, 2015. www.moma.org/collection/works/130571?locale=en.

NEW MEDIA AND ENGAGEMENT

Introduction: New Media Beyond an Art Medium

Walker Art Center – Museum Key Note at the 2012 MuseumNext Conference. Accessed: July 28, 2013. vimeo.com/44162636.

"Why anthropologists should study news media." 2010. Oslo, antropologi.info social anthropology in the news blog. Accessed October 18, 2012. antropologi.info/blog/anthropology/2010/why-anthropologists-should-study-news.

Benjamin, Walter. "The Work of Art in the Age of Its Technological Reproducibility: Second Version" in *The Work of Art in the Age of its Technological Reproducibility and Other Writings on Media,* edited by Jennings, Michael, et al. 19–55. Belknap Press of Harvard University Press, Cambridge, MA, 2008.

Curran, James and Gurevitch, Michael eds. 1991. *Mass Media and Society.* London, Edward Arnold.

Grimshaw, Anna and Ravetz, Amanda eds. 2005. *Visualizing Anthropology.* Bristol, Intellect Books.

Lovejoy, Margot 2004. *Digital Currents Art in the Electronic Age.* New York, Routledge.

Pink, Sarah ed. 2012. *Advances in Visual Methodology.* London, Sage Publications Ltd.

Standford Encyclopedia of Philosophy. 2011. "Walter Benjamin." The Metaphysics Research Lab, Center for the Study of Language and Information, Stanford University. Accessed November 30, 2016. plato.stanford.edu/entries/benjamin/.

Quaranta, Domenico. 2012. "What's (Really) Specific about New Media Art? Curating in the Information Age." New York City, Rhizome Blog. Accessed December 18, 2012. rhizome.org/editorial/2012/dec/6/whats-really-specific-about-new-media-art-curating/.

Stevenson, Nick. 1995. *Understanding Media Cultures.* London, Sage Publications.

Svensson, Patrik. 2010. "The Landscape of Digital Humanities." digital humanities quarterly, vol. 4, no. 1. Accessed Oct. 13, 2014. digitalhumanities.org/dhq/vol/4/1/000080/000080.html.

A Blog as an Artist's Workspace

Hertz, Garnet. 1995. "The Godfather of Technology and Art: An interview with Billy Kluver." Vancouver, Canada. Accessed July 10, 2013. conceptlab.com/interviews/kluver.html.

Edinger, Carrie. 2013. "Introduction to December 2013 Posts." Accessed December 12, 2013. carrieidaedinger.blogspot.com/2013/12/introduction-to-december-2013-posts.html.

Edinger, Carrie. 2013. "A Blog as an Artist's Workspace." Accessed: December 12, 2013. carrieidaedinger.blogspot.com/2013/12/a-blog-as-artists-workspace-introduction.html.

Edinger, Carrie. 2013. "02 Blogging as a Postmodern Artist Tool." Accessed December 13, 2013. carrieidaedinger.blogspot.com/2013/12/02-blogging-as-postmodern-artist-tool.html.

Edinger, Carrie. 2013. "03 The Structure of the Blog." Accessed December 14, 2013. carrieidaedinger.blogspot.com/2013/12/03-structure-of-blog.html.

Edinger, Carrie. 2013. "04 Video Research, An Example of the Blog's Layout." Accessed December 15, 2013. carrieidaedinger.blogspot.com/2013/12/04-video-research-example-of-blogs.html.

Edinger, Carrie. 2013. "05 Continuation- postmodernism and forming art-based research." Accessed December 16, 2013. carrieidaedinger.blogspot.com/2013/12/05-continuation-postmodernism-and.html.

Heleta, Savo. 2017. "Academics can change the world – if they stop talking to their peers." Accessed: September 16, 2017. theconversation.com/academics-can-change-the-world-if-they-stop-talking-only-to-their-peers-55713.

Kirby, Alan. 2006. "The Death of Postmodernism and Beyond." Accessed October 10, 2013. philosophynow.org/issues/58/The_Death_of_Postmodernism_And_Beyond.

Kirkup Gill. 2010. "Academic Blogging, Academic Practice, and Academic Identity," in *London Review of Education.* vol. 8, no. 1, pp. 75 – 84.

Lovejoy, Margot. 1989. *Postmodern Currents Art and Artists in the Age of Electronic Media.* Ann Arbor, UMI Research Press.

Lovejoy, Margot. 1992. *Second Edition Postmodern Currents Art and Artists in the Age of Electronic Media.* Englewood Cliffs, Prentice-Hall.

Lovejoy, Margot. 2004. *Digital Currents: Art in the Electronic Age.* New York, Routledge.

Nardi, Bonnie, et al. 2004. "Why We Blog." Communications of the ACM 47, no. 12.

Refsum, Grete. 2002. "Contribution to an Understanding of the Knowledge Base in the Field of Visual Arts." Working Papers in Art and Design 2 Retrieved 2013 from URL herts.ac.uk/__data/assets/pdf_file/0014/12308/WPIAAD_vol2_refsum.pdf. ISSN 1466-4917

Seidman, Steven. 1994. *The Postmodern Turn New Perspectives on Social Theory*. Cambridge, Cambridge University Press.

Sullivan, Graeme. 2005. *Art Practice as Research*. London, Sage Publications.

Varnelis, Kazys. "The Immediated Now: Network Culture and the Poetics of Reality." networked a (networked_book about (networked_art). Accessed December 26, 2016. varnelis.networkedbook.org/the-immediated-now-network-culture-and-the-poetics-of-reality/.

Varnelis, Kazys. 2010. "The meaning of network culture (1)." openDemocracy. Accessed December 26, 2016. opendemocracy.net/kazys-varnelis/meaning-of-network-culture-1.

Video as Research

Edinger, Carrie. 2013. "Video Research and Interdisciplinary Practice." Accessed April 13, 2013. carrieidaedinger.blogspot.com/2013/04/video-research-and-interdisciplinary.html.

Edinger, Carrie. 2013 "Video as Research with a 60 Second Time-Frame." Accessed July 27, 2013. carrieidaedinger.blogspot.com/2013/07/video-as-research-with-60-second-time.html.

Edinger, Carrie. 2015. "Mouth Collection and Continued Investigation with Sound." Accessed April 2, 2015. carrieidaedinger.blogspot.com/2015/04/mouth-collection-and-continued.html.

Khan, Jawad. "5 Ways Video Can Make Your Content Marketing Strategy More Effective." Business.com. Accessed: July 28, 2016. business.com/articles/5-ways-video-can-make-your-content-marketing-strategy-more-effective/.

Kirkup Gill. 2010. "Academic Blogging, Academic Practice, and Academic Identity," in *London Review of Education*. vol. 8, no. 1, pp. 75 – 84.

Lovejoy, Margot. 1989. *Postmodern Currents Art and Artists in the Age of Electronic Media*. Ann Arbor, UMI Research Press.

Lovejoy, Margot. 1992. *Second Edition Postmodern Currents Art and Artists in the Age of Electronic Media*. Englewood Cliffs, Prentice-Hall.

Lovejoy, Margot. 2004. *Digital Currents: Art in the Electronic Age*. New York, Routledge.

Pink, Sarah. 2001. *Visual Ethnography*. London, SAGE Publications Inc.

Pink, Sarah. 2012. *Advances in Visual Methodology*. London, SAGE Publications Inc.

Rush, Michael. 2007. *Video Art*. London, Thames & Hudson.

Russell, Carl. 1999. *Experimental Ethnography The Work of Film in the Age of Video*. Durham, Duke University Press.

Wright Christopher. 2010. "In the Thick of It: Notes on Observation and Context," in *Between Art and Anthropology*, edited by Arnd Schneider & Christopher Wright. Oxford, Berg.

Social Media and Public Accessibility

Carrie Ida Edinger's official tumblr blog. "Public Bulletin Board Collections." Last modified July 2013. carrieidaedingercollection.tumblr.com.

Carrie Ida Edinger's official Facebook fan page. "Carrie Ida Edinger's Collections." Last modified May 2014. facebook.com/Carrie-Ida-Edingers-Collection-269354606467847/.

Carrie Ida Edinger's official Google plus page. "Carrie Ida Edinger's Collections." Last modified April 2013. plus.google.com/100724315631138669491.

Berners-Lee, Tim. 2010. "Long Live the Web: A Call for Continued Open Standards and Neutrality." New York, *Scientific American*. Accessed November 12, 2012. scientificamerican.com/article.cfm?id=long-live-the-web&page=2.

Berners-Lee, Tim. 2009. "The Next Web." TED Ideas worth spreading. Accessed November 14, 2012. ted.com/talks/tim_berners_lee_on_the_next_web.

Browne, Rachel. 2006. "Review of Kenneth E. Goodpaster Conscience and Corporate Culture." University of Sheffield, *Philosophy for Business*. Accessed April 10 2011. isfp.co.uk/businesspathways/issue32.html.

Edinger, Carrie. 2012. "Public Access and Social Media." Accessed February 17, 2012. carrieidaedinger.blogspot.com/2012/02/public-access-and-social-media.html.

Edinger, Carrie. 2012. "The Collection Project and Social Media's Role." Accessed November 25, 2012. carrieidaedinger.blogspot.com/2012/11/the-collection-project-and-social.html.

Edinger, Carrie. 2013. "Considering the 'content.' in Web Design." Accessed August 19, 2013. carrieidaedinger.blogspot.com/2013/08/considering-content-in-web-design.html.

Edinger, Carrie. 2013. "Social Media Page and LIMITS." Accessed September 15, 2013. carrieidaedinger.blogspot.com/2013/09/social-media-page-and-limits.html.

Edinger, Carrie. 2014. "Continuation of Social Media Page and LIMITS." Accessed May 21, 2014. carrieidaedinger.blogspot.com/2014/05/continuation-of-social-media-page-and.html.

Edinger, Carrie. 2014. "Social Media Connection Analysis and The Internet-based Collection Project." Accessed May 30, 2014. carrieidaedinger.blogspot.com/2014/05/social-media-connetion-anaysis-and.html.

Goodpaster, Kenneth. 2007. *Conscience and Corporate Culture*. Oxford, Blackwell.

Gray, L. 2012. "Facebook Launches Promoted Posts, Pay As Little As $5 For More Fans To See Page Content." New York, *SocialFresh*. Accessed November 18, 2012. socialfresh.com/facebook-promoted-posts-go-live/.

Peterson, Tim. 2012. "Facebook Rolling Out Pages-Only Feed." New York, *Adweek*. Accessed November 14, 2012. adweek.com/news/technology/facebook-rolling-out-pages-only-feed-145181#1.

Pickering, Ben. 2011. "Does Facebook Fan-Gating Hurt Facebook Engagement?" California, SocialMedia *Examiner*. Accessed November 14, 2012. socialmediaexaminer.com/does-facebook-fan-gating-hurt-facebook-engagement/.

Rinehart, Richard and Ippolito, Jon. 2014. *Re-collection Art, New Media, and Social Memory*. Cambridge, The MIT Press.

Sydell, Laura. 2014. "FCC To Unveil Proposed Rules To Govern Internet Traffic." Washington D.C., NPR. Accessed May 15, 2014. npr.org/blogs/alltechconsidered/2014/05/15/312666733/fcc-to-unveil-proposed-rulesto-govern-internet-traffic.

The Digital and Social of Net.Art

Bishop, Claire. 2006. *Participation*. London, Whitechapel.

Bishop, Claire. 2014. *Radical Museology*. London, Koenig.

Bosma, Josephine. 2011. *Nettitudes Let's Talk Net Art*. Rotterdam, NAi Publishers.

Goriunova, Olga. 2012. *Art Platforms and Cultural Production on the Internet*. New York, Routledge.

Graham, Beryl ed. 2014. *New Collecting: exhibiting and audiences after new media art*. Surrey, England; Ashgate.

Rinehart, Richard and Ippolito, Jon. 2014. *Re-collection Art, New Media, and Social Memory*. Cambridge, The MIT Press.

Conclusion An Artist's Response to "Criticism"

Barrett, Estelle and Bolt, Barbara eds. 2007. *Practice as Research Approaches to Creative Arts Enquiry*. London, I.B. Tauris & Co. LTD.

Foster, Hal. 1995. "The Artist as Ethnographer?", in *The Traffic in Culture Refiguring Art and Anthropology*. edited by George Marcus and Fred Myers, 302–309 Berkeley, University of California Press.

Foster, Hal. 1996. *The Return of the Real*. Cambridge, MIT Press.

McLean, Athena and Leibing, Annette eds. 2007. *The Shadow Side of Fieldwork*. Oxford, Blackwell Publishing.

Okely, Judith and Callaway, Ann Hampton eds. 1992. *Anthropology & Autobiography*. London, Routledge.

Stiles Kristine. 1996. "General Introduction," in *Theories and Documents of Contemporary Art A Sourcebook of Artists' Writings*. Edited by Kristine Stiles and Peter Selz, 1–9 Berkeley: University of California Press.

Sullivan, Graeme. 2005. *Art Practice as Research*. London, Sage Publications.

Varnelis, Kazys. 2010. "The meaning of network culture (1)." openDemocracy. Accessed December 26, 2016. opendemocracy.net/kazys-varnelis/meaning-of-network-culture-1.

www.ingramcontent.com/pod-product-compliance
Lightning Source LLC
Chambersburg PA
CBHW040825180526
45159CB00001B/66